Sade's Wife

Madame DE LAUNAY, & Monſieur
le Préſident & Madame la Préſidente
DE MONTREUIL, ſont venus pour
avoir l'honneur de vous voir, & vous
faire part du Mariage de Mademoiſelle
DE MONTREUIL, leur petite-Fille
& Fille, avec Monſieur le Marquis
DE SADE.

Invitation to the marriage of Renée-Pélagie de Montreuil to the
Marquis de Sade, May 1763

Sade's Wife

The Woman behind the Marquis

Margaret Crosland

PETER OWEN
London & Chester Springs PA

PETER OWEN PUBLISHERS
73 Kenway Road London SW5 0RE
Peter Owen books are distributed in the USA by
Dufour Editions Inc. Chester Springs PA 19425–0007

First published in Great Britain 1995
© Margaret Crosland 1995

The photograph of the Château de La Coste
(by Nguyen Tien Lap) on the back of
the book jacket is taken from *La Coste
en Provence* by Henri Fauville (Aix-en-Provence:
Edisud, 1984) with the permission of the publishers.

ISBN 0–7206–0958–5

A catalogue record for this book is available from
the British Library

Printed and made in Great Britain by Biddles
of Guildford and King's Lynn

Preface

Sade's wife? Did he have one? Who was she? The woman who contracted an arranged marriage with the young Marquis de Sade in 1763, a few months before he became known for extremist sexual behaviour, has not been ignored by his biographers but has remained an enigmatic figure who stood shadowed at his side for nearly thirty years.

As with her husband, we do not know what she looked like, for the absence of family portraits has only deepened the enigma of the Sade ménage. A portrait of the Marquis's father has survived, and a possible likeness of his mother. But in the case of his wife and himself, we are fortunate enough to hear instead their voices, which reach us clearly in their long exchanges of letters with each other and with a few other people. These documents, patiently edited and analysed by the scholars and biographers listed in the bibliography of the present book, reveal in detail the more than unusual life of this unique couple. More particularly we also learn how one woman, in a century when women possessed sexual power but few legal rights of their own, defied a dominant mother in her desperate attempts to help the difficult man she so unaccountably loved, before and during the confused times of the French Revolution: until suddenly she could not tolerate him any longer and retired into Christian-orientated solitude.

*

Preface

I have been greatly helped in the writing of this book by General (Vicomte) Pierre Lesquen du Plessis Casso, a descendant of the Sade-Montreuil-Menildurand families, by my persevering researcher Denise Merlin and by my editor Michael Levien.

I should also like to thank Jeffrey Simmons, the University of London Library, the London Library, Kent County Council Arts and Libraries, Sabrina Izzard and her staff at Hall's Bookshop, Tunbridge Wells, and Mike Ridley.

Margaret Crosland

Contents

The front endpapers reproduce parts of two letters from the Marquise to her husband, 20 August 1787 (*left*) and 29 December 1788 (*right*).

The back endpapers reproduce parts of a letter from the Marquis de Sade to his wife, April 1784.

(From *Lettres et Mélanges littéraires écrits à Vincennes et à la Bastille, etc.,* ed. G. Daumas and G. Lely, Editions Borderie, 1980)

Prologue

In the summer of 1778 a woman of thirty-seven, living in Paris, wrote a short letter to her husband, sending it to his lawyer who would deliver it to him when it was safe to do so. It was not safe for the time being, for her husband, she knew or at least hoped, was just about to escape from prison. If he had already escaped, no one would know where he was. 'Do you believe now,' she wrote, 'that I love you, my dear little friend, whom I adore a thousand times over? Take good care of your health, don't go short of anything.'

They had been married fifteen years, they had three children, he had been in prison four times and the escape now being planned or already achieved, was his second. His wife, who had helped in the planning, did not yet know that it would be short-lived. She was deeply in love with her husband and in this letter she addressed him as *tu* (they both tended to use *vous* more than *tu*). She was desperate for news and equally desperate that nothing should go wrong: '. . . have letters written to me in someone else's handwriting and between the lines write to me in invisible ink'. She intended to do likewise; she would join him when she could and explain many things. He was not to worry about anything, she was on tenterhooks until she received some news. 'But I would rather have no news than that you should take risks.' His lawyer would give him as much money as he wanted. 'Take care of yourself, I entreat you. . . .'

Somehow she had scraped together some money for him, but he perpetually complained that he never had enough, for which he blamed either the lawyer or his wife herself. In fact he blamed her for most things, but he constantly needed her, if only to receive his complaints: she was the Marquise de Sade.

How had she come to hold that title?

1 *Dutiful Daughter*

Matrimony is sometimes convenient, but never delightful. – *La Rochefoucauld*

Renée-Pélagie de Montreuil, born in France in 1741, had known since the age of ten or so what kind of future awaited her: a husband would be found for her, preferably a member of a higher social class, a marriage would be arranged, a contract drawn up concerning property and money; she would then spend the rest of her life bringing up her children, supervising their education and generally conducting the social life of her family. Any sons would probably go into the army, suitable husbands would be found for the daughters. Her own mother had lived this way; there was no possibility of a change to the system. Her mother, Marie-Madeleine Masson de Plissay, daughter of a royal counsellor, had been married in 1720 to Claude-René Cordier de Launay de Montreuil, a lawyer who had been successful enough to become honorary president, later president, of the Cour des Aides in Paris. He belonged to the class of non-aristocratic nobility known as the *noblesse de robe*, or in a slightly derogatory sense, the *robinocratie*, and could be considered a good match, for there was no shortage of money and the likelihood of increased professional and social success. The Montreuil couple had five or possibly six children. They could be described as rich, comfortable and no doubt happy.

Claude-René was known as *le Président*, and his wife, who was to play an important part in this story, was *la Présidente*.

Marie-Madeleine's parents may not have known just how 'suitable' for her this husband was, for she was such a born organizer that he became the invisible man. Presumably Claude-René Cordier was dedicated to his professional work. He had bought a house in the rue Neuve-du-Luxembourg, a fashionable part of Paris, forming the modern rue Cambon, and the Château d'Echauffour in Normandy. His father had purchased the château in 1720 and when Claude-René acquired it twenty years later he styled himself Cordier de Montreuil. Later the family acquired other châteaux: Vallery near Sens, and Verrières in the Yvelines.

The Montreuil family might seem to have had no problems, and they did not expect any difficulty when they applied their minds to the future of their eldest daughter, Renée-Pélagie, who in 1762 was already twenty-one, quite old enough for marriage. In fact many girls were married at a much younger age. If Renée had been a great beauty or possessed any obvious feminine appeal, maybe her parents would already have received applications from interested families, for the Montreuils could offer a good match from the financial point of view, the most important aspect of the arrangement which was regarded as a business deal. This eldest daughter, however, was no beauty. She was not tall, she had brown hair and grey eyes, tended to walk like a man and was not interested in attractive clothes. Very few details of her physical appearance are ever mentioned and no authentic portrait of her has survived. One that has sometimes been reproduced is thought more likely to show her mother-in-law. In 1901 Paul Ginisty, using unidentified evidence, evoked her presence: 'She was not precisely beautiful; her face, illuminated by bright eyes, was gentle, expressive, and had a certain timid grace beneath which could be sensed a depth of passion, indicating a warm and vibrant soul, not yet aware of itself.' He continued with a mention of her background and a foretaste of her future: 'Her youthful existence had in fact been passed in a strict atmosphere under the supervision of an authoritarian mother and had been extremely quiet. She was the kind of woman whom a superficial glance can declare indifferent while attentive observation would have discerned on the contrary both interesting features, a mixture of clumsiness and decision, a gaze of extreme frankness and a concentrated fire.'

It can be assumed that she was brought up and educated like all the young women of her class in the mid-eighteenth century. In France this was a century of paradox, for if now it seems dominated by images of women, these same women, painted by Boucher, Fragonard, Greuze, Lancret and many others, could wield personal and even political power but had no civil rights. Among the aristocrats and the middle classes that power was in the first place sexuality, always emphasized against a background of physical beauty, discreet intelligence and high culture. Among working women sexuality controlled power of a different kind: prostitution augmented the low incomes on which they struggled to survive, and it has been estimated that one woman in every seven was engaged in some aspect of the vice trade. This was a century when the bourgeoise Jeanne-Antoinette Poisson, otherwise Madame de Pompadour, could become *maîtresse en titre* to King Louis XV and retain the role for nearly forty years. She, like Queen Marie-Antoinette later, had infinitely more glamour than the kings with whom they were associated, and in their different ways they played important, if not always helpful, roles in the government of the country. Yet their partners, to use a late-twentieth-century term, could have dismissed them at any time if they so wished.

Through another paradox the *philosophes* who made this the century of the Enlightenment were hardly concerned with the rights of women, only with the rights of man. Contributors to the *Encyclopédie* were more preoccupied by the physiology of women than by their social independence, and if earlier writers, such as Montesquieu, had observed women with perceptive wit, only the brilliant and fair-minded Condorcet among Renée-Pélagie's contemporaries seems to have thought of them as potentially equal to men. During the previous century

Poulain de la Barre had attempted to show, by the application of Cartesian principles, that women were logically the equal of men. His book *De l'égalité des deux sexes* was published in 1673, and during the following year he brought out *De l'éducation des dames*, but these pioneering titles were not constructively followed up in the next century. The *philosophes*, including the intelligent Diderot, were happy to profit from the salons, all conducted by women, but, again with the exception of Condorcet, they barely considered these people, who had developed a special kind of skill, particularly useful to writers and thinkers, as individuals in their own right.

Admittedly most of the avant-garde among these male *philosophes* believed that women should be better educated, but with one purpose: in this way they would be more entertaining wives and mistresses, and some of them at least might buy books.

So Renée-Pélagie de Montreuil would receive most of her education in the orthodox contemporary way, at a convent. There the nuns would teach her how to love God and, through the precepts of the Christian faith, she would learn to be a good wife and mother. Strangely perhaps, it was during the previous century that more detailed attention had been paid to the education of girls, and as far back as 1678 Fénelon, Archbishop of Cambrai, had published his reasonable and still readable book *De l'éducation des filles*. He and his followers were keen to remind teachers – that is, mainly clerics, nuns and parents – that girls should be encouraged to read but never allowed any books which might inflame their too-vivid imagination. Convent education was obviously limited because the nuns could teach their charges about faith and forgiveness, but about the practical side of life, and more especially of married life, they could teach nothing, for they had no experience of it. Only one precept was clear: a wife must be submissive to her husband.

Of Renée-Pélagie's education nothing is known, but her parents, after her early years at the chosen convent, would surely have employed all the resources of private tutors. It was essential for her to learn all the social graces, dancing, singing, even amateur acting, popular among the aristocrats and the better off. A private theatre was a sign of social success. This was the training that fitted a girl for her career, the career of marriage, for outside the Church there was virtually no other. Her mother, Madame de Montreuil, must have had a highly expensive education herself, for she was intelligent enough to deserve it and without it she could never have written over twenty years or so those skilful and compelling letters which were matched only by one other writer who was to enter the family: her future son-in-law. Her daughter wrote good letters in a different way, never long letters, but she never learnt to spell.

In 1762 or early in the following year Madame de Montreuil began to look for this son-in-law. Since she always followed the social rules, she was determined that her eldest daughter should be married first, and she was equally determined that this marriage should endow the family with something they did not possess, something they could not buy. She wanted the next generation of Montreuils to be upwardly mobile, to move beyond the *noblesse de robe* to the *noblesse d'épée*, the true aristocracy named 'of the sword' because it had been based, down the centuries, on rewards granted by the monarch to military leaders whose prowess in battle had brought glory to France. If one could not buy aristocracy, there was one way of entering this privileged group, indirectly, and that was through a well-organized marriage.

Through her husband's profession, her own inherited money and her compelling personality Madame de Montreuil already had many powerful friends, some of them close to the court, but for her that was not enough. She wanted to enter the charmed circle, the aristocracy, through any means available. She naturally mentioned to members of her family that she was beginning to think about a husband for her daughter. There is no evidence that the family drew up a list of possible partners and examined their various credentials, because one name was put forward remarkably soon.

La Présidente's uncle, Jean Partyet, who had earlier worked in Cadiz as commercial representative for the French Government, was now superintendent in charge of the war veterans, *les invalides*. He mentioned to the people he met that a husband was being sought for his great niece, who had become twenty-one in December 1762. One man in particular listened carefully to what he said. Jean-Baptiste Joseph François, Comte de Sade, was more than anxious to find a wife for his only son, Donatien-Alphonse-François, Marquis de Sade, who would eventually inherit his father's old title and all that went with it. If Madame de Montreuil hoped to fulfil some of her own ambitions through her daughter's marriage, the Comte also had ambitions, but they were of a different kind. In the first place he himself was deeply in debt, apparently through gambling and general incompetence, and needed money. Secondly, he could not deal with his son who had been discharged from the army at the end of the Seven Years War in 1763 and was now leading a crazy life of time-wasting enjoyment, running up even more debts. The Comte did not even pretend to love his son, he merely wanted to be rid of him. Despite an early career in diplomacy the Comte, while representing his country at the court of the Elector of Saxony, had behaved with some dishonesty. His wife, Marie Eléonore de Maillé de Carman, who came of a distinguished family and was distantly related to the King, had decided to live apart from her husband in a Carmelite convent. Whether she did this to save money or to prevent marital unhappiness is not clear. The Comte complained to his brother the Abbé de Sade and to everyone else he could think of that he himself was poverty-stricken and ill while his son took no notice of his plight and did not interrupt his balls, theatre parties and country outings or picnics in order to visit him.

The Comte had already considered one possible bride and, even though she was the daugther of a Florentine banker, he rejected her because he had soon discovered the Montreuils to be richer. The Sades were a very old and truly aristocratic family with much property in Provence, where most branches of the family lived. In one sense the Comte was isolated, separated from his wife, living far from his older brothers, his more interesting brother the Abbé de Sade, as well as from his four sisters, all of whom, except one, were nuns and also lived in Provence. His son not only neglected him, his riotous behaviour was causing scandal in Paris, the debts were mounting on all sides and soon it might be too late – no family would accept a young man who had nothing to offer beyond a title and a bad reputation. Thus the Comte became more and more interested in the Montreuils.

If Renée-Pélagie had been educated like all girls of her class, she had also been brought up by two parents in what was no doubt a secure home. Her possible future husband had known a very different kind of youth, even if he also had received the type of education chosen by many families of his class. The Comte and Comtesse were absent parents, often travelling abroad with their eminent employer, the Prince de Condé and his wife. As a result, their young son was sent first to his uncle the Abbé de Sade in Provence, where he was on his own admission spoilt by his grandmother. He was in touch with his various aunts, one of whom was married and had a daughter, while he also had a governess, Madame de Saint-Germain, whom he respected greatly and never forgot. He escaped briefly from this woman-dominated life when he was sent, at the age of ten, to the Collège Louis-le-Grand in Paris, run by the Jesuits. They taught him well and accustomed him to grim physical conditions, such as poor food and dirty rooms. At the same time all the students were encouraged to take part in plays; but they also had to accept the homosexual practices for which the Jesuits were notorious.

By 1764 the members of the Society of Jesus were expelled from France, mainly for political reasons. The young Marquis acquired a tutor, the Abbé Amblet, who remained one of Sade's few friends as he grew older. Then came seven years in the army, which he joined at the age of fifteen. There had not been much time for 'normal' life. Was it surprising, as the French signed the humiliating Peace of Paris in 1763, by which the country lost most of its overseas empire, that the young officers who could now see no future for themselves and little for France, decided to direct their energies into having a good time? What or who could give them any sense of responsibility, especially when members of the royal family failed to show any and the mismanagement of the Seven Years War had been mainly due to aristocratic military leaders who were simply not professional enough?

If Renée-Pélagie de Montreuil, leading a sheltered life in the rue Neuve-du-Luxembourg, had succeeded in reading any of those romantic tales so deplored by Fénelon and others, she had seen nothing of the world, and she would certainly not have been allowed the slightest chance of any relationship, even a salon flirtation, with any man. Madame de Montreuil would have taken good care that such a thing should never happen, for all daughters must be preserved from any hint of scandal. Daughters were highly saleable objects; each one had her price.

The young Sade, however, at twenty-two, was experienced in many different types of relationship. He had bought prostitutes and camp-followers, although he regretted that the best payers were given the best times, but most of all he had developed a talent for falling dramatically in love. Shortly before he left the army he had met a young woman of thirty or so in Hesdin, in the north of the country, and appointed her as his fiancée. He was at the time involved in amateur theatricals, and his would-be romantic attachment seems to have been part of the performance. However, this episode was closed when he had to travel to Provence following the death of his grandmother.

Early in 1763 those two very different families, the Sades and the Montreuils, seemed to be moving closer together and the Comte had been pleased to discover that behind the Montreuil parents there was an older generation likely to bequeath some very useful money to Renée-Pélagie. Her parents announced that they were prepared to house and maintain the young couple for five years, and the Comte became more interested at each new proposition. He still worried incessantly, he felt poorer every day. '[H]ow can we have a wedding this year,' he wrote to his brother the Abbé, 'since we have nothing. We should need a carriage.'

What he needed most of all was some co-operation from his son, which was not forthcoming. While the two families were planning the future of their two young people, unmindful of any feelings the daughter and son might have on the subject, the Marquis fell desperately in love with a girl of his own class, Laure-Victoire Adeline de Lauris, who came of a Provençal family like himself. They seem to have lived together and in the passionate letters Sade wrote to her (he kept copies) there are mysterious references to what seems to have been some venereal disease. There had been talk of an engagement, approaches to the girl's father, romantic declarations by the Marquis and fury from the Comte. The Montreuil parents did not know much about this at first, but they must have found it odd that the prospective bridegroom showed no enthusiasm for returning to Paris, for he had gone back to Provence to be close to Laure.

Before long, gossip spread from Provence, but the Montreuils were so keen to pursue the planned marriage that they did not allow themselves to be deterred by a young man who was merely, they thought, sowing his wild oats with the main purpose of defying his father.

Renée-Pélagie had apparently had sight of the man she was to marry, but she seems to have had an unconscious rival in her own family. When the Marquis first came to see her she was apparently indisposed. Instead he saw her younger sister Anne-Prospère and was immediately attracted to her. She was only twelve at the time, and Sade's request to marry her instead of Renée-Pélagie was brushed aside. She must have looked older than her years, but if the story is apocryphal later developments prove that it may have been more than a biographical rumour. However, Madame de Montreuil insisted that according to tradition the eldest daughter must be married first.

During April 1763 the marriage became urgent, mainly because the Comte was terrified the deal would escape him, his mounting debts could not be settled and his infuriating son would still be on his hands. He knew that the Montreuils had begun to hear gossip about the Marquis's reckless behaviour and at all costs be must get the young man back to Paris. This young man could hardly have been more reluctant, seeing himself no doubt as a romantic hero forced to give up true love for the commands of family duty. Like Edward Gibbon a year later, reluctantly giving up his love for Suzanne Curchod, he 'sighed as a lover' and 'obeyed as a son'. The Montreuils were told that he was convalescing from a fever, and while the Comte grumbled about the expense of the journey the bridegroom seems to have reached Paris the day before the marriage contract was signed. If he had not arrived, the result would have been a humiliating disaster for both families – one seeking money, the other social promotion. Since the Sades were members of the aristocracy, the King himself had to approve the marriage and had already done so, even if the bridegroom had not attended that particular ceremony. Madame de Montreuil was ready to feel extremely proud of herself. If Renée-Pélagie was feeling pleased or apprehensive or excited, her feelings did not matter.

The Comte de Sade liked his son's future in-laws; in fact he had to like them. On 19 April 1763 he told his sister, the Abbesse de Saint-Laurent, about the Sunday when he had dined with them. 'They are the best and most honourable people in the world and everyone says that my son is very fortunate to join this family. I feel very sorry for them because they are making such a bad acquisition, someone capable of doing all kinds of stupid things.' He was pleased that Laure de Lauris in Provence had told the Marquis she did not want him. He went on to describe the Montreuils: 'On Sunday I didn't find *la petite* ugly. She has a very pretty bosom, her arms and hands are very white, and there's nothing about her that shocks, nothing, she has a delightful nature.' He went on to describe her parents: 'Her mother is very likeable, amusing and gay. The father is a very good man, full of *probité*.'

The Comte was delighted with these generous people who had even agreed to lend him money (against a surety) for the wedding ceremony: this money would provide suitable clothing for the Marquis and his servants and also buy him a carriage and two horses. The Comte received no co-operation from his own wife, the Comtesse, who had not only refused to donate her diamonds as part of the marriage settlement but had avoided the Sunday gathering by pretending to be ill. She would apparently have preferred to see her son married to Laure de Lauris and had refused for a long time to sign the necessary papers for the Montreuil contract. The Comte had described her as 'a terrible woman, my son will take after her'. If she signed eventually, it is clear from the family correspondence that she distanced herself from the whole arrangement and that Renée-Pélagie was unlikely to suffer from an interfering mother-in-law.

Her own mother, however, had to employ a great deal of skill and patience in negotiating with Renée's future father-in-law. The Comte had cleverly avoided paying anything towards the cost of the wedding. He had made one grand gesture four years earlier which had cost him nothing either: he had given up his title as lieutenant-general to four provinces in favour of his son, who was designated in the marriage contract as due to receive the revenues this arrangement produced. However, by 1763 the Comte had paid nothing and this led to family disagreement.

But this is to anticipate. The unwilling bridegroom had eventually returned to Paris, bringing with him, as requested by his father, 'two or three dozen artichokes' which would form a useful (and cheap) contribution towards the wedding celebrations. Also he was to bring either a tunny-fish pâté, or, according to another deciphering of the relevant letter (from the Comte, presumably to one of his sisters), some thyme.

Eventually, then, the two people most concerned in these marriage arrangements, the Comte de Sade and Madame de Montreuil, were satisfied, despite the problems of finance and the Marquis's bad reputation. The contract was signed, its many pages containing a large number of eminent names and among them all one name and designation notable for their simplicity: 'Demoiselle Anne-Prospère de Launay, sister'.

The following day, 17 May, the religious ceremony took place at the now vanished church of Sainte-Marie-Madeleine in the parish of Ville-l'Évêque, near the Montreuil home. Until Sade's biographer Maurice Lever learnt this detail from the official marriage records it had always been thought that the ceremony took place in the splendid and fashionable church of Saint-Roch, in the rue Saint-Honoré. Known today as the 'actors' church', this would have been a suitable venue. But like so many places that might have been associated with this story, the building where this marriage of opposites was consecrated no longer exists. No details are known about the ceremony but many grand personages attended, including the Duc de Richelieu.

How did the innocent young woman and the highly experienced young man react to the new situation, the legal link that bound their lives together? Of Renée-Pélagie's reaction nothing is known, but her husband was ready to tell his uncle the Abbé at least something about the life he had not wanted but knew he must accept. Surprisingly perhaps marriage to Renée-Pélagie was more enjoyable than he had expected: 'By the same post, my dear uncle,' he wrote, 'you will receive a letter from my wife. I cannot praise her enough. I am equally delighted by my father-in-law and my mother-in-law: they apply themselves to my interests with incredible warmth. I had only been vaguely aware of all the advantages of my new existence. All I can tell you about it is that I am delighted.' Everyone else was delighted too and surprised, for, the Abbé noted, 'the young lady is not pretty'.

She had, however, survived the shock of her new life. She probably knew nothing at all about the sexual side of marriage, although her mother, at forty-three, presumably still lived a sexual life, and her youngest child was barely three years old at the time of her daughter's marriage. At this stage of the eighteenth century girls of the Montreuil class were told nothing until the day before the wedding, and girls like Renée-

Pélagie would never have been allowed to see obscene books or prints, which provided education for many, especially for people who could not read. In one of his stories 'L'époux complaisant' ('The Obliging Husband'), written some twenty years later, Sade referred to the ignorance of girls: 'He had been given in marriage to a very inexperienced girl and, in accordance with the custom, she had only been given information the previous day....' The mother had even found it indecent to mention certain details. The story was no more than a farce, but in later serious moments Sade attacked the system of arranged marriages. The newly-weds did not leave Paris for some romantic honeymoon, but they enjoyed themselves, especially at the theatre. They may not have been aware that the old Comte spied on them, to make certain that his wayward son was not letting the side down. He was generous enough to take the pair to dinner near the Château de Marly and reported to his brother all that was happening. Madame de Montreuil accepted all the Marquis's *fantaisies*, he wrote; she was 'crazy about him. Within the family they don't recognize her any more'. But his son was empty-headed and only wanted pleasure, which he could find nowhere. He would not make proper visits or carry out any duties, he had not called on his father, whereas Madame de Montreuil came to see him every day.

Perhaps the Comte was not prepared for her next step, for if he had found her lively and amusing he had perhaps not realized how dangerous she could be where questions of money and family honour were concerned. Barely ten days after the wedding she began writing to the Abbé de Sade, letters full of flattery and superficially humble respect. She referred to the *douceur* of her daughter's character, 'her attachment to her husband and the wish to please both him, and the house to which she has the honour to belong', but she skilfully hinted at a problem which had come to light: the Comte had not paid his son the revenues from the provinces he had earlier given up on his behalf. Four years' money was owing and the Comte was not ready to pay it, saying he had supported his son during the intervening period. It is not clear if or how this problem was settled, but discussion of it showed clearly who was running the family. The Comte probably paid in the end, for he said he wanted nothing more to do with his son.

When Renée-Pélagie wrote to her uncle by marriage she presumably penned short, polite letters saying nothing or very little. In early June she had been presented at court, thus beginning to fulfil some of la Présidente's ambitions. She may have guessed that her mother was telling the Abbé everything, having found him infinitely more receptive than his depressed, depressing and apparently mean-spirited brother. Her mother told the Abbé that she had 'entrusted' her daughter to the Marquis, but she still described him as 'so young, so young', emphasizing no doubt that if he had had experience of a sort in the army he did not know much about adult life in what she saw as the 'normal' world. One thing worried her, and the young couple, a little: her daughter did not seem to be pregnant yet. But she assured the Abbé, who may not have cared too much, that she was not impatient, for neither side of the family showed any signs of sterility. This letter was written on 14 September 1763 from the Château d'Echauffour in Normandy.

The following month she reminded the Abbé how much her daughter looked forward to meeting him and how much she loved her husband. That was easy, for he was lovable. 'So far he loves her very much, he treats her very well.' Renée-Pélagie was at that moment very sad, for her husband, *le drôle d'enfant*, as la Présidente called him, had gone briefly to Paris, he was to go to court at Fontainebleau (he hated court visits) and was to see the Duc de Choiseul, the King's most active minister, about a possible post.

If any honeymoon period can be difficult, that following an arranged marriage might be even more difficult still, and in this case there had been no time for the couple to become acquainted. But had they, coming from such different backgrounds, unaccountably experienced what Montaigne had advised: 'A good marriage, if there be any such, rejects the company and conditions of love, and tries to represent those of friend-ship.'? Sade himself was no doubt happy because at last he was aware of family support from the Montreuils, and not just financial security. There had been little support of any kind during his twenty-three years to date. Admittedly there had been other children within reach of Saumane, where he had lived with his uncle the Abbé, there had been companions at the Collège and in the army, but there had been no true family circle and all his life Sade was notably short of friends. An only child is usually delighted to be suddenly a member of a large united family.

At the risk of sounding sentimental, he needed love, all the more so because he was impossibly difficult to love, and his father had soon convinced himself that he was not worth the effort. Renée-Pélagie had at least known security, but she was not her mother's favourite daughter and a child is always aware of such preferences. That favourite was to enter the story later. At the same time the daughter of an authoritarian mother surely had to make an escape somehow, but in the mid-eighteenth century such a girl could not easily take up a career or run away from home in a romantic elopement. Renée-Pélagie needed to escape by loving someone, and in her husband she found someone who had probably never received any love, although he was no doubt unaware of the fact. While sexually he was an experienced man, emotionally he was a child, as his mother-in-law had so soon discovered, telling the Abbé how she scolded him sometimes. There were other factors too. In 1762 Rousseau had published *Émile*, in which he set out his theories of edu-cation. He invented the perfect feminine companion for his ideally educated young man: this was Sophie, who in all things must remain submissive; any independence on her past was to be carefully limited. Sade was a great admirer of Rousseau, but even if he had not yet read the book he seemed unexpec-tedly to have found in Renée-Pélagie a ready-made Sophie.

Also, this young wife was a Christian. She had been brought up in the faith and the vows she had made in church surely meant more to her than the terms of the utterly materialistic marriage contract. As for her husband, who had been brought up principally by professional clerics, he at least accepted, for the time being, an atmosphere that was welcoming but one from which he could not easily escape.

For the time being: but that time was not very long.

2 Protective Wife

Is it, in heav'n, a crime to love too well? – *Alexander Pope*

It was probably in August, three months after the wedding, that the Montreuil family left Paris for the Château d'Echauffour. The edifice dated from the Middle Ages and had once been the most highly defended English-owned fortress in northern France. In the mid-eighteenth century, however, it was an ideal country house for privileged people who could afford the staff needed to run it. It had previously been neglected, since the owners had not lived there, and the Montreuils had worked hard to make it habitable. Elegant marble or stone *cheminées* were installed in every room, and metal plaques were affixed to them display the combined coats of arms of the new occupants. These devices appeared also in the home farm and the gardener's cottage, although not in the main château kitchen. The Cordier de Montreuil arms were *d'azur au chevron d'or accompagné de trois croissants d'argent*, while the Masson de Plissay *écu* fitted neatly alongside: *d'azur au chevron d'or accompagné de deux étoiles en chef et d'un croissant en pointe, le tout d'argent*. Such a display might have sounded typical of *nouveaux riches* but in fact Renée-Pélagie's parents were not the first generation to have made money: her mother's family had grown rich through trading with India and still owned manufacturing activities in Orléans.

Madame de Montreuil did not go to Echauffour to relax, for that was something she never did. In fact she never stopped writing letters to the Abbé de Sade, informing him of domestic news and feeling constantly pleased that she had promoted her daughter, but principally herself, into a noble family. Did she ever take her eyes off the young couple? It seems unlikely. There are no records of outings they may have made together, but there may have been amateur theatricals, organized of course by Sade, for he immediately involved all his in-laws in these entertainments. He was organized in his turn, when he was not reading or sleeping, his 'two certain resources', and he was putting on weight. He went out stag-hunting, doubtless unaccompanied by his wife, while his father-in-law took him to visit the Cistercian abbey of La Grande Trappe, which, according to Madame de Montreuil, was only three leagues away. 'He was very keen on this trip, not to stay there, I think' (her idea of a joke, perhaps), and she hoped he would find it edifying. Neither she nor Renée-Pélagie would have joined this expedition, for women were not allowed to visit the Trappists. Madame de Montreuil would not have been interested in the vow of silence, if she was as talkative as her letters seem to prove. Her daughter probably reacted by talking little, and later on, when she became a letter-writer in her turn, she rarely wrote long ones and did not care for long words.

It was la Présidente, inevitably, who began to spread the word in December 1763 about the young wife's hoped-for pregnancy, which seems to have dated from September, but during the months of waiting a great deal, much had happened. On 20 October Madame de Montreuil told the Abbé in detail about recent progress in family relationships. Her quarrels with her son-in-law never lasted long, she said, and if he was scatterbrained, marriage would cure that. Her daughter would never scold him, she wrote, for she loved him totally, and that was easy, for he was lovable. He was now away in Paris, hopeful that he might have news of some military or administrative post.

Did his wife or mother-in-law wonder if he would seek out his favourite libertine entertainments in Paris? La Présidente, a great realist, may have suspected it, for she had already told the Abbé how the tranquillity of country life might not satisfy 'his mind and his tastes, they are lively, and need nourishment'.

If Renée-Pélagie loved her husband, as she clearly did, she probably expressed her love emotionally rather than sexually. She did not refuse her husband, they both wanted children, but she was apparently cold, at least during this early stage of her marriage. A year earlier the Comte de Sade had referred to his son as 'combustible', and that is what he was. He needed violent sex, and if he demanded any such within marriage it was still married sex, which was part of a different dimension, less exciting. It is known from later correspondence that the couple practised anal sex, but that age-old practice could not be called violent.

Nearly twenty years later, in June 1783, Sade wrote cheerfully to his wife recalling their good times, contrasting their practices with those of the Montreuils, whose sexuality allegedly took place only in the 'vessel of propagation', according to Jansenist doctrine, whereas he believed in what the Jesuits and the Cartesians had taught him: one must not 'swim in the void', 'nature abhors a vacuum', but she, Renée-Pélagie, was 'a philosopher; you have another very good way of conducting the matter, another narrow way and warmth in the rectum which gives me a strong reason for agreeing with you'.

The two women remaining in Normandy that autumn might have expected Sade to enjoy himself in Paris, but they would not have expected to learn the events of the 18–19 October which took place in a small rented house somewhere beyond the rue Mouffetard, now in the 5th arrondissement. Sade's night with the girl called Jeanne Testard expressed in microcosm his state of mind, especially in reaction to his marriage, plus the social situation in Paris eleven years before the death of Louis XV, twenty-five years before the Revolution. Like thousands of other working girls Jeanne Testard needed to supplement her earnings – she was a fan-maker – and prostitution, through a procuress or *madame*, was the obvious way to go about it, even if it could often be dangerous. For her it was surely the only way. She would have known in advance that she might be asked to take part in flagellation practices, favoured by libertines for centuries, and particularly popular in Paris at this time. Some girls would refuse to whip or be whipped, and their clients would have to find another diversion or another girl. This particular girl was upset when she was warned of a surprise that awaited her, for she claimed she was pregnant and did not want a shock of any sort. However, out of sheer terror she took part in a disgusting display of sacrilege and impiety, was forced to look at obscene prints on the wall and, strangest of all, she was forced to listen to this strange young man reading obscene verses to her. She was rescued by the procuress next morning and at once went to the police, although her client had naïvely hoped she would keep her promise of silence. In her complaint she gave the authorities every possible detail about this man except his name, which she did not know. He was at once identified, other prostitutes came forward, his conduct was reported to Fontainebleau, subsequent reports to the King recommended severe punishment and on 29 October Sade was imprisoned at Vincennes.

It can be assumed that Madame de Montreuil was quickly informed of the situation, because among her useful friends was the Lieutenant-General of Police, Antoine de Sartine. It is not clear how much she told Renée-Pélagie, for the latter in her pregnant state might have suffered a miscarriage. The little fan-maker, if she had been telling the truth, had been aware of the same problem, but she had co-operated because she was desperate to avoid further trouble.

If the prisoner did not feel guilty he tried very hard to sound so, writing pathetic letters to Sartine asking for one single consolation, begging him to inform his wife of his 'wretched state'. He knew she would be worried about him, for by now he had been away from Echauffour for over ten days without any explanation. 'Nothing can equal the anxiety she must be feeling, receiving no more news of me.' He had written to his mother-in-law, he said, but in case this letter had not been sent on, could Monsieur Sartine please write to her himself. He was obviously nervous about the terms of any such letter; he hoped the police chief would 'say only what you judge to be *à propos*', and later he made it clear what he meant by this: 'I hope, Monsieur, that you will be good enough not to inform my family of the real reason for my detention, I should be lost without hope in their eyes.' He said that he had visited the house beyond the rue Mouffetard only in June and referred to 'the unfortunate book', which seemed to contain incriminating evidence, either the obscene verses he had read to the girl (maybe he had written them, but this has remained a mystery) or else the book, or notebook, gave away dates of other assignments or sexual exploits in this house with relevant details. In the rest of the letter he may have been writing as a total hypocrite or he may have been sincerely thinking of his wife, for he wrote in terms which she would have understood. He appeared to be a sinner repenting of his sins: 'In no way do I complain of my fate; I deserved the vengeance of God, I am undergoing it; my sole occupation is to lament my faults and detest my sins.' He asked to see a priest, he sincerely repented and hoped he would soon be in a position to approach 'the divine sacraments, the total neglect of which had become the first cause of my downfall'. His wife was constantly in his mind, he wrote to the authorities, desperately hoping to see 'the person who is more dear to me than anyone in the world. If you knew her you would see that her conversation more than anything else is capable of restoring to the right path an unhappy man who is in total despair at having turned away from it'. Had he attended mass regularly, as his wife and family surely did? The old church of Saint-André was not far from the château. If he attended for the sake of form he was not alone, for even the atheist Duc de Choiseul did so, it was part of politically correct behaviour. If Voltaire and the *encyclopédistes* had been hoping for a long time to secularize France their campaign was still far from won, and if everyone was aware of abuses by the clergy, blasphemy and impiety could still be severely punished. In 1766, for instance, the Chevalier de La Barre, aged only nineteen, was cruelly executed for these 'crimes'.

Nothing would have upset Renée-Pélagie more than the disgusting acts of impiety carried out with the terrified little fanmaker in the house near the rue Mouffetard. They have been described briefly here because most of them were concealed from his wife. In future she was to know everything. Her husband's behaviour in the autumn of 1763 could probably be interpreted as an indirect attack on his conventional in-laws, and even on the wife who throughout her existence remained at least superficially devout. He could possibly have been exasperated by the dull country life of Normandy – his mother-in-law called it tranquillity – and his reading of obscene poems satisfied that lifelong need for an audience.

As things worked out, it was the dull country life which he now exchanged for Paris and the prison at Vincennes. It is not clear how the Comte de Sade heard what had happened, but the father who was barely on speaking terms with his son now took action. Perhaps he remembered some melodramatic incidents from his own youth, but in any case he sped to Fontainebleau, grumbling about the expense, and thanks perhaps to the diplomatic skills he had once exercised, he persuaded the King to release his son from Vincennes after only two weeks. There is no doubt that the Montreuils also exerted pressure and this double use of privilege at aristocratic and professional levels could not be ignored. The Comte at once developed a fever and said he was very unhappy. The Marquis was restored to his wife because he was to be punished by a form of house arrest. He was to remain at Echauffour until further orders, and his adopted family would watch over him. His mother-in-law informed the Abbé of the situation: his nephew would now have to make up for the past by 'irreproachable conduct in the future. Since he has been restored to us we are satisfied'. She pointed out that she and her husband had done for him only what they would do for a son of their own. It is clear that Renée-Pélagie had not been kept utterly in the dark: 'As for my daughter, you can understand her suffering. She has behaved like a virtuous wife.' She was about three months pregnant when this letter was written and apart from sickness she was fairly well. Since the family had to stay at Echauffour to supervise the erring husband, they told their Paris friends that they were there because of Renée-Pélagie's eventual *accouchement*. Her mother assured the Abbé that this was an excuse, the young woman was too 'delicate' for this event to take place in the country, the château was too far from any place offering suitable medical attention. The girl's father-in-law, the Comte, had hoped his son would visit the Provençal Château de La Coste, which was already his in principle, and Renée wanted to go with him, as soon as he was free from his 'detention', but her husband said the journey would be impossible for her in her present state.

The Marquis was released from house arrest, at least temporarily, in early May and must have been ready to escape from the 'tranquillity' of Normandy. A heavily pregnant wife was no companion and he possibly hoped that if he went away briefly he would find a new-born son or daughter on his return. He went not to La Coste but to Dijon, taking up the governership of the four provinces which his father had passed over to him. He soon returned, and if he was looking forward secretly to more of his preferred entertainments in Paris he knew he must at least make a show of respectability for the time being.

Sadly, the first Sade baby, born probably in April or early May, lived only briefly and the disappointed mother recovered slowly. The Marquis filled in the next few weeks with his favourite activity, producing plays, this time in the private theatre at the Château d'Evry, owned by the Marquis de Brunet d'Evry, who had married one of la Présidente's sisters. Amateur acting had been elevated into an art form by Madame de Pompadour and her friends; it amused the King and had become high fashion. Among the long list of plays given at Evry was one which ended with songs, written by Sade, celebrating the fact that his recent bad behaviour was now forgiven. The play was called

L'avocat Patelin, he was 'Valère' and Renée was 'Henriette'. In six lines Valère (it is known that the Marquis had a pleasant singing voice) recalled that 'happiness had been far away, but now it was in his heart, now he was constant'. The last two lines were hopeful and moralistic:

> *Il ne faut s'étonner de rien:*
> *Il n'est qu'un pas du mal au bien.*

Renée-Pélagie, presumably recovered now from six months of unhappy events, the discovery of her husband's 'crimes', his imprisonment, his house arrest and the loss of their child, sang lines which were even more hopeful:

> *Cher Valère, on sent le danger*
> *Quand d'amour on sent la puissance;*
> *Mais je ne redoute plus rien:*
> *Passons vite du mal au bien.*

Perhaps there was more meaning to these deceptively simple lines than was apparent to the audience. The 'power of love' had indeed been dangerous to Renée-Pélagie, for she had been unsuspecting and then too forgiving, perhaps. Had she any faith now in what her husband made her sing, did she really no longer 'fear anything'? If he was not a great lyric writer he was clever enough to end her lines with an echo of the phrase given to Valère – that is, himself: 'Let us move quickly from bad to good.' It was Madame de Montreuil herself who sang the last of the eight verses, some of which expressed the happiness of family feeling, virtue and friendship. The author might even have been thinking of Rousseau.

Perhaps the family, especially Renée-Pélagie and her mother, believed all the trouble was over, something that was easy for Renée, for she had clearly begun to love her husband with that perfect love which casteth out fear. If she had been disconcerted by the presence of Inspector Marais, who haunted the château and was to prove a useful spy for her mother, she could not complain and probably didn't. La Présidente, however, found plenty to complain about during the next few years, for if her son-in-law committed no crime as such he treated his wife badly with his frequent absences in Paris. He had realized that it would be better not to indulge in violent sex for the time being. Instead, he chose to live through violent emotions and 'normal' sex and for that reason spent his time with actresses instead of prostitutes. In any case brothel-keepers had been warned not to supply him with girls, but many of the young women he now professed to adore had merely taken one step upwards from the streets to the theatre, and they were all mercenary. His mother-in-law, defending her half-abandoned daughter and the family honour, used Inspector Marais to report on the time and money the Marquis wasted on these girls and claimed that she had personally separated him from one of them. She probably meant that she had paid Marais or his acolytes to do it.

The young man could never have enough emotional excitement and became experienced in writing melodramatic love-letters. Their writing was probably more meaningful to him than the girls themselves, so much so that he often kept copies. Writing was beginning to obsess him just as much as sex.

However mercenary the actresses and dancers, they were courtesans not street-girls. Their admirers did not whip them, but proved their love by buying expensive presents or paying the rent. It is perhaps unlikely that Renée-Pélagie ever saw, or even heard of, a letter her husband wrote to his uncle the Abbé in September 1765. The Abbé had reproached him for not visiting him while in Provence, but his nephew replied that he had been told his uncle did not want him: for he was not alone. He was with an attractive young woman called Mademoiselle de Beauvoisin, formerly of the Opéra, so attractive that aristocrats competed for her favours and were prepared to pay high prices for them. On the whole she preferred Sade. Like Renée-Pélagie she was ready to give up a great deal for this inexplicable man, at least for the time being.

Sade put forward all possible excuses for his behaviour. He had been spending vast sums of money which he did not have in creating a theatre at Château de La Coste and had taken la Beauvoisin with him. He had even, it was rumoured, let it be understood that she was the Marquise herself. At this date nobody in Provence, not even the Abbé, had ever seen the true Marquise. If la Beauvoisin was prepared to play the part, and she probably was, there is no proof that she usurped Renée-Pélagie's place for any length of time and of course the Marquis later denied any such attempt. In any case, he was not rich enough for the actress; she merely enjoyed the dalliance, while he no doubt imagined himself as a *jeune premier* appearing on a half-built stage accompanied by a young woman who was more attractive than his wife. He told his uncle he would always love him, but what he wrote next might have led even his adoring wife to reject him.

'Yes,' he went on, 'I should no doubt be happier if I loved my wife, but am I in control of that feeling, I've done all I could, my dear uncle, to overcome the repugnance which I felt for her from the first moment, I have never succeeded, who knew better than you how I was married, in what circumstances, was it the time to withdraw when I arrived in Paris; all the preparations had been made, the King had signed, something which has never been done without the presence of the future husband, which was noticed by the whole of Paris!'

He was surely the first bridegroom who had failed to attend this important ceremony, but the two families had decided to proceed without him, as though he did not really matter. The money, and therefore the power of decision, belonged to the Montreuils.

The Marquis went on to describe how he had acted out the part expected of him: 'I did what in truth an honourable man should never do, my mouth made promises that my heart could not keep.' But that was not all. He ceased to believe himself committed because only outward form was involved: 'I believed that my entire duty consisted in hiding my true feelings.' For a time the disguising of his 'hatred' made him feel less weighed down by duty, he was tired of constraint and 'having for two years said "I love you" without thinking it; I tried to think it in order to feel pleasure in saying it'. Had he really played the hypocrite for two whole years? 'I saw clearly then, but in reproaching myself for having been a deceiver, I planned to deceive even more.'

He moaned to his uncle that he was more to be pitied than blamed, told him not to mention this letter to anyone and thanked him for the understanding letters he had written to his mother-in-law. He had seen some of them. However, a year later the situation became even more confused. While writing to his uncle again about money, his father's health and his uncle's book, he asked for one favour: that he should forget 'the errors committed during the blindness of a passion which I could not control, you must believe that the proofs that were wickedly and unwisely placed in your hands were written only at the dictation of the Siren who had turned my head'. He alleged that the passion was over. He implied, but did not say, that he did not hate his wife; neither did he say that he loved her. 'Restored to myself, I would have been incapable of such conduct and now that the illusion has completely gone I blush at what happened and cannot believe it.'

Was the young man a complete liar and hypocrite or does the letter simply prove what later became obvious, that he was surrounded all his life by women who in their different ways always had power over him? Presumably la Beauvoisin had dictated the letter, but earlier that year he had written to another woman referring to 'an unhappy alliance, dictated by money' which had brought nothing but 'thorns'.

It should be noted that Sade found few interesting men friends with whom to correspond. With exceptions such as his old tutor, his various professional agents, his lawyer and so forth, such men were virtually absent from his life. He preferred the company of his valets. Neither did this particular 'illusion' disappear as quickly as he alleged. La Beauvoisin appeared briefly again in his life and then, before she finally vanished, she made a grand gesture, selling some of her jewellery and giving the money to Sade. Did she share something with Renée-Pélagie, even on a short-term basis? Did she find the man irresistible, forgivable?

Meanwhile his mother-in-law, who knew every detail of this liaison – '*c'est une phrenesie*,' she wrote, with picturesque spelling – from the police and maybe even from specially appointed spies in Provence, continued to correspond with the Abbé, hoping that he would do something or even say something to restrain his nephew and help her daughter. The Abbé was thought to have attended theatricals or celebrations at La Coste and failed to complain about the presence of the actress. Did he not realize the humiliation of the young Marquise? The Abbé, however, was still counselling patience and pointing out that the Comte his brother had used all the wrong methods in attempting to cope with his son's long-lasting adolescence.

Madame de Montreuil now began to utter threats, always of course on behalf of her suffering and silent daughter. One begins to wonder if this daughter was grateful for her mother's attitude or if she was beginning to find it more exhausting than helpful. The Abbé tried to console la Présidente by recounting what he had learnt through a recent visit from his nephew: 'I spoke to him a great deal about his wife, as you can imagine. He is aware of all her worth; he praised her a great deal; he feels friendship for her and much respect; if he displeased her he would be in despair, but he finds her too cold and too pious for him, and that is why he seeks entertainment elsewhere.' The Abbé was sure that when he had passed *l'âge bouillant des passions*, 'he will realize the value of the wife you have given him'. And the Abbé repeated what Sade himself had told him in 1763: 'He said that his wife was unaware of his follies, and that he would be in despair if she knew about them: that is something.'

But there could be blackmail within the family. 'The young man,' wrote his mother-in-law, 'can be sure that just as I have co-operated in concealing his stupid acts from his wife or excusing them in order not to alienate the two of them' (she could have come dangerously close to doing so) 'then I shall be just as firm in telling her about them and convincing her of her unfortunate destiny when that becomes necessary in order to preserve her from greater misfortunes in perpetuating her mistake.' She would be forced to tell Renée-Pélagie everything unless Sade's behaviour showed 'a sudden change, of which he is not capable'.

Yet Sade was more fortunate than he knew. Renée-Pélagie also, for the time being at least, was not capable of 'sincere change'. No behaviour by her husband, however bad, would affect the uncritical, near-maternal love she felt for him.

Late in 1766 she was pregnant again. Early the following year her father-in-law the Comte de Sade died and his son showed such grief that even the critical Présidente was moved by what seemed to be sincere regret. She thought that after all he must be capable of family feeling and she felt quite reconciled to him. Louis-Marie de Sade was born in Paris at the end of August 1767, everyone was pleased, even if the child's father did not arrive from La Coste, where the villagers had been paying homage to their new seigneur, until this first heir was a few days old. Even the Dowager Comtesse de Sade emerged from her convent for the baptism, held in the chapel of the Hôtel de Condé where she herself had been married in 1734 and her own son baptized in 1740. Louis-Marie had two aristocratic godparents: the Prince de Condé and the Princesse de Conti. Madame de Montreuil must have felt that her social ambitions were satisfied, even if the price paid so far had been embarrassingly high.

Renée-Pélagie's husband was now officially Comte de Sade, but he did not use the title and rarely did so later. He was preoccupied with the work he had initiated at La Coste, using money he did not have and concentrating on the theatre he longed to see finished, but at least he seemed to be thinking of family life there, and he began to concentrate on the design and decoration of an apartment for his wife.

According to Henri Fauville, historian of La Coste, these new quarters were 'furnished in better taste than the rest of the château'. Had Renée-Pélagie been consulted, or was her husband trying to make amends for his recent infidelities? She was to have four rooms, a boudoir, papered in grey and green, patterned with landscapes, and there was a carpet in the same colours, the only carpet mentioned in the inventories. The little winter bedroom had a bed with a canopy and the walls were in a yellow shade of orange; while the summer bedroom was larger, its walls hung with blue moiré silk. There was, too, a splendid bathroom in the château, with a copper bath and boiler, and the general hygienic arrangements included fifteen *chaises percées* and six bidets. Renée-Pélagie was also allotted a little bureau, but her favourite living-room later was to be the 'little green salon' which contained a marble-topped walnut chest of drawers on which stood 'a large tortoise-shell clock . . . surmounted by a savage holding a lance in one hand and a shield in the other'. Renée's husband obviously saw her as a hostess receiving many guests, and there was plenty of accommodation for them. There were forty-two rooms in all, while the dining-room contained six tables, a tric-trac (backgammon) table, twenty-two chairs, mirrors, chandeliers, a tapestry mounted on green leather and four large pictures. In addition, there was a big *salle de compagnie* with a marble chimney-piece and a gaming table, the windows curtained in patterned chintz with a white ground.

No wonder the costs escalated and the Marquise received many of the accounts, which her husband seemed to hope she, or her mother, might pay. She was not to see La Coste for a few years yet, but she was evidently growing into her true role. The birth of her first son, the Sade heir, seems to have given her new confidence, and if she allowed her mother or her mother's staff to bring up her child, as was usual at the time, she began to act on her own. The worse her husband's behaviour, the more responsible she seemed to become, the more insistent on supporting him, forgiving him, accepting what the police called *horreurs*. There was no shortage in the mid-1760s of *horreurs* committed by the French aristocracy and accepted as more or less normal. Since the Peace of Paris in 1763 the despotic monarchy had continued virtually unchanged.

Louis XV wept as Madame de Pompadour's funeral cortège passed by in 1764, and Choiseul planned the marriage of the Dauphin and Marie-Antoinette of Austria.

Students of sadism have paid much attention to the events of Easter Day, 3 April 1768, the day when the Marquis took Rose Keller, a thirty-six-year-old widow, to the *petite maison* which he rented at Arcueil, south of Paris on the way to Sceaux. He beat her, she claimed he wounded her with a knife, then rubbed wax into the wounds. She escaped, refused money and complained to the police. It is not clear how the Montreuil household was informed, but Renée and her parents knew there was no time to be wasted. Too many witnesses had listened to Rose Keller, it would not be easy to silence everyone this time, but the Montreuils immediately invoked one of the privileges available on application to the King – the *lettre de cachet*, which removed any alleged wrongdoer from the jurisdiction of the courts and dispatched him 'safely' to gaol. By 8 April Sade was consigned to the Château de Saumur and his wife had already shown a great deal of foresight. On 7 April she had summoned one of the very few friends her husband possessed, his tutor the Abbé Amblet from the Collège Louis-le-Grand days, and sent him to Arcueil. He came back from the *petite maison* with the silver and some prints she had asked him to rescue. There was also a mysterious wardrobe key that he must find, but it is not clear if he did. The true purpose of his visit was of course to make sure there was no incriminating evidence in the house, no instruments of torture, no *malheureux livre* or its equivalent. Sade's valet might have cleaned the place up after the 'victim' had escaped. This victim was not ready to suffer any more at the hands of privileged people and demanded a large sum of money. Madame de Montreuil sent Amblet and a lawyer to bargain with Rose Keller, and the bargain was hard. Sade was bitter about this settlement. Years later he was still complaining to his wife that the woman had been paid far too much, that she was a prostitute, and why all this trouble over *le cul d'une putain*?

If Keller was not a prostitute, she had obviously been naïve

when arriving at Arcueil. If Renée-Pélagie had been naïve, no
doubt because of the way her mother tried to run her life, she
had now matured: if she knew or didn't know about her husband's behaviour, she was prepared for anything. Naturally
she needed her parents' help in coping with the legal aspects
of this latest problem, but it had been she who had sent Amblet
to Arcueil and now she paid off the rent of the *petite maison*
at Arcueil: her husband could never use it again. In the same
way she terminated the arrangements for a house he had been
using at Versailles.

The many legal complexities that ended the Rose Keller affair and the way in which privilege and money narrowly won
the day belong to the biography of Sade, but Renée-Pélagie
was herself deeply involved now; she did not leave everything
to her mother as she done in 1763. She knew that Chancellor
Maupéou had a grudge against her father which may have led
to a dangerous revenge; she was humiliated when bailiffs were
sent to search the apartments she shared with her husband.
She saw the story taken up by the gazette writers, the gossips
and the foreign press. In England Horace Walpole was informed
about it by Madame du Deffand as early as 12 April. Renée-
Pélagie could not doubt her husband's guilt, and must have
been horrified by the choice of Easter Day, but like her mother
she may have tried to play the story down. She saw two other
women come to her husband's defence: her own mother-in-
law, the Dowager Comtesse de Sade, normally so silent, and
his former governess, Madame de Saint-Germain. Apart from
the Abbé Amblet, no men had come forward.

While her mother was as usual complaining to the Abbé
about his nephew, she was probably also complaining to her
daughter about her behaviour, because suddenly she was faced
with a young woman who seemed to have changed. In fact
she had not changed, she had merely passed suddenly from a
passive existence to an active one, all conditioned by the same
unvaried feelings for her husband. 'Wherever Donatien was,'
wrote Jean-Jacques Pauvert in 1986, 'she had to be there. If
Donatien was suffering, she had to intervene.'

Her mother had written to the Abbé at the end of April that it was easy to imagine the sufferings of her daughter. The only consolation within the family was her little son. He was well and his first teeth were just about to come through. Renée-Pélagie's first thoughts all the same were for her husband. In April, not even three weeks after that disastrous Easter Day, Madame de Sade was writing to the authorities at Versailles asking for the prisoner to be allowed fresh air and more privileges generally – although he was far from ill-treated – and help from a servant in caring for the fistula from which he was suffering. She had moderate success, and that only determined her on even firmer action. She was barely twenty-six at the time and had probably done nothing so far without her mother's urging or permission. Certainly she had no experience in writing to government departments or prison governors.

But now la Présidente found she was acting out of character, she could hardly believe what was happening, for her daughter began to conceal things from her, she became deeply involved in her husband's endless debts and went to see one of his financial advisers without consulting her mother. And there was worse: she had to see her husband, come what may. She was impelled to go to Lyon, for he had now been transferred to the prison of Pierre-Encise which was not far away from that town. How was she to find the money for the journey? 'I learnt,' wrote her mother to the Abbé a little later, 'although she tried to conceal the fact from me, that she sold the few diamonds she possessed for this journey.' She had also agreed to give her mother-in-law the Dowager Comtesse the pension that her husband was due to pay since his father's death. Sade of course had no money for this, since he was spending more than he possessed on high living and luxury building at La Coste – he had been unexpectedly released from prison in November provided he stayed at the château and kept away from Paris and Echauffour.

In the meantime, however, his wife had stayed in Lyon and visited him as much as possible, often in private, and by September she was again pregnant. There had earlier been a plan that she would go with her husband to La Coste but in the end she went back to Paris, probably because she wanted to do all she could to sort out her husband's disastrous financial affairs. She knew he was doing nothing about them, and if she had gone with him to Provence she would certainly have failed to stop him spending even more money. When he was released in November 1768 her mother had wanted her to go, saying that she had done so much by now that she should complete her work 'by giving [her husband] all possible marks of attachment'. La Présidente was obviously relieved: Sade had been released so quickly without too much scandal in the end that she was again optimistic about the family's future. 'Your great nephew is very well,' she told the Abbé, 'and walks entirely on his own [little Louis-Marie was about eighteen months old now], he is very good-looking; I care for him with all the affection I have for her father and mother.' Perhaps she hoped to please the Abbé by mentioning her son-in-law before her daughter, who by now was almost a stranger to her.

But by March 1769 pessimism crept in again. The two women had agreed together that Sade should now conceal his 'past dissipations' and try to clear his debts. There was a chance that he could return to the army – which soon evaporated – but why did not Sade co-operate in any way? Why did he want to disobey the King by leaving La Coste and not paying his debts? Renée-Pélagie understood. That was his contrary nature; it would not change. He had been willing to accept the advantages of privilege but he wanted, unconsciously so far, to show that social conventions meant nothing to him; it was his long-term ambition to destroy them. If a loving wife understood, for everything her husband thought and did was acceptable to her, a conventional and ambitious mother-in-law did not. She now told the Abbé that she was abandoning her son-in-law to him. 'As for me, I give up.' She was going to devote herself to her daughter and her unhappy children. Louis-Marie was very well. Although she was a prejudiced grandmother, she again stressed his good looks and said that 'he often kisses his daddy's portrait in his mother's bedroom. I confess that it breaks my heart'. Madame de Montreuil knew exactly when and how to introduce an emotional note into her tough, money-centred letters to the Abbé.

Renée-Pélagie's pregnancy continued, although her worries affected her general health, she had a sore throat and 'over-heated blood', but it was her husband's health that preoccupied her most. She had succeeded in gaining permission for him to live briefly near Paris in order to find good medical attention for his fistula. Otherwise he could not return to the army, as everyone hoped he would.

Donatien-Claude-Armand was born on 27 June 1769, a 'big, strong boy', and if his mother could not sleep and her blood was still overheated, at least his father came to Paris and tried to behave like a good husband and father. It was a politic course of action. He wanted his wife to join him at La Coste, but her parents were far from keen. The Marquis must learn that he could not make everyone tremble before him by uttering 'Je veux'. But he still asserted his rights and would not give his wife legal authority to deal with financial problems on his behalf. He was mean about household expenses but she, as a married woman, had no rights at all. At one point la Présidente had even mentioned separation, but maybe that was her idea alone, developed or talked about during low moments. Renée-Pélagie was not thinking about separation. With help from her parents she had struggled to save this selfish young man from long imprisonment and a judgement which would have destroyed two families and their children. Possible revenge from the legal profession, which had turned Sade into a scapegoat, had been in the end defeated by the autocratic power of the King, supported obviously by appeals to his officials, appeals from women.

Renée-Pélagie, who was to continue appealing on her husband's behalf for the next twenty years, doubtless saw no further than her personal situation, but this virtual escape from justice by a privileged person was part of the process which eventually came to destroy the French aristocracy. Louis XV and his ministers still assumed they could perpetuate the despotic authority of the King's great-grandfather, Louis XIV, but

the behaviour of too many aristocrats, especially when it en-
tailed the ill-treatment of women, had begun to shock the non-
aristocrats, the Third Estate. Could nothing be done to stop
it? Louis XV was entertained by the police reports of scandals
but he was not concerned enough with punishment when the
culprits were close to him. The Comte de Charolais, for instance, a grandson of le Grand Condé, behaved so badly, ruth-
lessly killing people for his own amusement and indulging in
the sexual torture of women, that his own family disowned
him. But he was not punished. His grandmother had been a
daughter of Louis XIV and his mistress Madame de Montespan:
the Comte knew that he was beyond the reach of the law.

Licentious and even cruel behaviour was not limited to men.
Various women, usually aristocrats, were also said to hire the
petites maisons for their own sexual games, and after all Choderlos
de Laclos, when he wrote *Les liaisons dangereuses*, surely had
various models for his corrupt heroine, Madame de Merteuil.

The activities of Renée-Pélagie's husband were small-time
horreurs, but they still helped to endanger his own class and
that of the Montreuils. The *ancien régime* could inflict cruel
punishments on non-aristocrats, and Robert-François Damiens,
who had attempted to assassinate the King in 1757, was hor-
ribly tortured to death: the guillotine, the instant killer, had
not yet been perfected in France. The *régime* found it easier to
send writers, who were mostly middle class, to prison if they
were guilty of alleged libel or sedition. Voltaire was in the
Bastille on two occasions and Diderot would have followed
him, but the Bastille on that occasion was full, so Diderot
went to Vincennes. Eventually Sade would find himself in both
prisons, but that lay far ahead.

The 'big strong boy' Claude-Armand was two months old
when his father left him and his mother to go on a tour of
Holland and Flanders. He later told the Abbé Amblet that he
had earned money for his sexual pleasures with an erotic book,
which was probably published in The Hague or Amsterdam.
He may also have had a play produced or merely read in Bordeaux and another in Lyon or Marseille. No news of any scandal

reached his wife, he was with her in 1770, and on 17 April 1771 their last child, Madeleine-Laure, was born. Strangely, perhaps, Madame de Montreuil was not in Paris with her daughter at the time, but at the Château de Vallery in the Yonne, another of the Montreuil possessions. She announced the birth to the Abbé, indicating that she was retained at Vallery on some 'indispensable' business. She was sad not to be with her daughter, 'But such is her destiny and mine; one must submit to it as to everything that does not depend on us.' She then launched unexpectedly into a description of her daughter: 'When she has the honour of being known to you, Monsieur, and to Monsieur de Sade's family, I hope that she will earn their true interest at least through her reason and her gentleness; one's appearance and graces are gifts from nature which one cannot control.' Was she trying to excuse her daughter's plainness? 'We have a little girl.... Endow her with your intelligence; I shall give her patience: I think it is the virtue most necessary to women.'

Madame de Montreuil, in taking the traditional view, no doubt spoke from the heart. She then added a postscript, saying that she would always share with pleasure 'all favourable matters affecting Monsieur de Sade. His interests are inseparable from those of his wife and children'. She was keen now to prove that she had not 'given up' her son-in-law and was determined to keep the Abbé on her side. She ended, as she often did, on an emotional note and proved that she had a favourite among her grandchildren as she had among her own daughters, as was proved later. 'Your great nephew, the elder, is the most handsome creature possible. The younger one interests me less; he is good-looking, but neither his mind nor his character are known yet; he is barely talking.' She then lapsed into nostalgia for the better moments of the bad old times: 'And then, the elder boy was in my arms, in my keeping during such unhappy moments... that he inspired me with a more tender concern....' He had been barely eight months old when his mother and grandmother had been devastated by the Rose Keller case. If she thought the bad old times were over, she could not have been more wrong.

3 Understanding Sister

In married life three is company and two is none. – *Oscar Wilde*

In the autumn of 1771 Renée-Pélagie saw for the first time the château where she now expected to live, probably for years, with her husband and children, many miles away at last from her authoritarian mother and the bad memories of those two horrifying episodes in Paris which had almost destroyed two families. About the first she had not known everything, but of the second she had known only too much, even if she could still congratulate herself on her own role as partial rescuer. It was a long way in every respect from the back streets of Paris, the little house at Arcueil, the courts, the prisons and, on a different social level, the Montreuil house in the rue Neuve-du-Luxembourg, over four hundred miles away.

In the Vaucluse department of Provence, west of Apt, southeast of Avignon, the château, today partly restored, still stands on a hill overlooking the village of La Coste on one side and the vast plain of the Lubéron on the other. There had been a fortified camp at this splendid site as far back as the eleventh century, a château was built there later and in 1627 it passed into the ownership of Jean-Baptiste de Sade of Saumane when he married Diane de Simiane. Her father was seigneur of La Coste and it was normal for the property to become that of her husband. Each successive owner, including Jean-Baptiste, Comte de Sade, developed and improved the château. The Marquis, operating always on credit, now committed a fortune on the interior and had also planned to develop the gardens, asking the staff to plant fruit trees, to care for the paths and organize farmyard stock, presumably rabbits and poultry. He hoped that he and his family could literally live off the land.

Renée-Pélagie had three children under five and probably little experience of housekeeping. Fortunately she had a nurse-governess to look after the children and she appointed a young woman of thirty to whom she could delegate the day-to-day organization of La Coste. This useful housekeeper was known as Gothon Duffé, but her real and grand-sounding name was Anne-Marguerite Maillefert. Like the majority of the Costains she was a Protestant. She had come from Switzerland and was later to play an unexpectedly important role in the life of the château and its inhabitants. She had one asset which fascinated any man who caught sight of her: she had a splendid bottom.

The chatelaine herself was immediately absorbed into her husband's activities, and he was now in his element, thinking only of his little theatre, the *salle de comédie* on the first floor, with its fixed scenery representing a salon which could easily be adapted into a variety of décors, its candle footlights, its blue curtain, its foyer. There were sixty seated places, while just as many spectators could stand at the back or in the gallery. Beyond the theatre was the terrace. At the cost of a myriad unpaid bills the Marquis had achieved his ambition: he could now happily exist in his dream-world and may even have thought that he would have no further need of adventures into fantasy living. Not content with the theatre at La Coste he was also building one at Mazan, the other Sade domain which stood some fifteen miles away to the north, east of Carpentras.

Renée-Pélagie, who had supported all her husband's plans, had already taken part in theatricals at his bidding and continued to do so now. She might have felt isolated among all the servants and the people whom Sade needed for his productions – professional actors and actresses, boys to put the candles out, a hairdresser-wigmaker, and even, apparently, local police officers in case of 'turbulence' during performances – but not long after the family's arrival they were joined by a guest who had not appeared in the story since she had signed the marriage contract in 1763.

This was Renée's younger sister, Anne-Prospère de Launay (she had been named after her mother's branch of the family), who had apparently been only twelve at the time of the wedding and was now barely twenty. Her parents had chosen to send her to a Benedictine convent near Lyon in the diocese of Clermont-Ferrand where normally only girls of aristocratic families were received, and she was now a *chanoinesse*, a nun who had not yet taken any vows and could if she wished choose not to take them. As a younger daughter she herself would probably have been given little choice in how she would spend her life, but it had presumably been decided that she deserved a good education.

Who had invited her to La Coste? If the sisters were in close touch Renée would have known that Anne-Prospère had been ill and needed to convalesce. Would the Marquis, remembering the pretty girl he had met in 1763, have suggested to his wife that she joined them? Would the younger sister have invited herself, or would la Présidente from Paris have suggested the visit? The most likely reason for her appearance is possibly an invitation from her sister, for otherwise Renée might have felt she had no support from her own family in this corner of Provence, a part of France she never came to like. The more she saw of the Costains too, the less she liked them, for she did not share their religion and could not accept their confrontational attitudes to any aspect of government or authority.

The younger sister made herself useful in the first place by establishing an inventory of all the lace and linen possessed by the current generation of the Sade family. She also met her uncle by marriage, the Abbé, and he seems to have been enchanted by her. La Présidente, in her non-stop letters to Saumane, had constantly commended her eldest daughter, for her virtue if not for her beauty. Now the Abbé had met her, presumably, but no documents have been published indicating how he reacted to the dutiful, understanding, rather plain young woman, his niece by marriage. On the other hand there is no shortage of evidence for his feelings about Anne-Prospère. He was about sixty-six, she about twenty, and they exchanged letters charmingly typical of eighteenth-century *galanterie*. Evidently she was well read and would have been quite capable of discussing with the Abbé the three-volume book he had written about Petrarch, published in 1764, the great poet who had so admired Laure de Sade in the fourteenth century. Anne-Prospère also played the lute. The Abbé was so fascinated that he gave her a useful gift, a Corsican pony, in the hope perhaps that she would ride over to Saumane, barely twenty miles away, to see him more often. She seems to have gone riding with the Marquis and she was persuaded to help him with secretarial work. Her health was not restored too quickly, for she wrote to Maître Fage, Sade's notary at the time, reminding him to send her the bathtub she needed: perhaps the elegant bathroom in the château was not yet finished, or was not suitable. She also pointed out that she needed to be in good health or she would not be able to act. The doctor came to see her from time to time, but even his bills do not explain the details of her health problem, except that in February she was suffering from a cold. Many tradesmen's bills have survived, and if many were left unpaid they still indicate that the thirty or so people living in the château during the winter to spring of 1771/2 did not go short of anything, everyone had shoes and boots made, while Renée-Pélagie acquired mules in pink drugget and Anne-Prospère had ordered pink silk drugget shoes. Certainly the whole family seem to have possessed a sweet tooth (this was to be the undoing of the Marquis later), for they consumed almond paste, much preserved fruit, jellies, jams and all sorts of other delicacies. But most time was spent either in the theatre or in some activity connected with it. The

Marquis acted as general director and producer, sometimes writing the plays himself, sometimes choosing classics or the plays he had already produced in the early years of his marriage.

In 1970 the Comte Xavier de Sade allowed the publication of some notes by his ancestor the Marquis relating to a play of his own entitled *Le mariage du siècle*. There were two cast lists, one of them including the professional actors and actresses whom Sade employed whenever he could, often acting with them himself, and the other assigning the roles to members of the family. In this play Anne-Prospère was given the part of the heroine, Pauline, while Renée-Pélagie had to be content with that of Sophie, who seems to have been merely a confidante. No doubt she was as usual uncomplaining, and one cannot see her as a dedicated amateur actress. Sade was nothing if not ambitious for his troupe, for he included in his repertoire plays by Voltaire, Régnard and Diderot, in addition to those which are now forgotten or known only to specialists.

That winter and spring provided plenty of excitement for the young people at La Coste, but not every member of the family was pleased. For instance Madame de Montreuil, far away in Paris, could not understand that her two daughters were too busy to write to her, rehearsing or performing or moving between the two theatres of La Coste and Mazan. She knew Anne-Prospère was with her sister and she knew, for she was always ready to pay for information, about their 'plays and entertainments'. She complained to the Abbé – he was never to escape her letters – that she did not know where her 'children' were. She was never more class-conscious than when she commented on the appearance of the professional actors, blaming of course her son-in-law. She complained that the behaviour of her own family had shocked the whole area by their appearance on the stage 'with people whose profession is to entertain those of the kind and condition of Monsieur de Sade when it suits both sides, but not to have the same standing in the eyes of the public'. She referred to the theatre as her son-in-law's 'dominating passion', his 'folly', and if he could do as he wished 'up to a certain point' she could not allow him to 'compromise further his wife and his sister-in-law'. She would put right this 'indignity', if he did not do so first. One did not sacrifice oneself in order to 'perpetuate extravagances'. She looked ahead to a gloomy future: 'When he has spent everything he will send me back the wife and children whom he hardly cares about, and I shall certainly receive them.' She saw only disaster in store for him, and he was not destined for that, she thought. He had only himself to blame, but why did his wife not restrain him?

Madame de Montreuil was not the only person to react critically to the Marquis's behaviour. The Abbé even confided in Maître Fage, who was no doubt trying to deal with creditors: 'I think as you do about my nephew's passion for acting which, as you see, is taken to extremes and would soon ruin him if it lasts. I have said nothing to him so far about this because I could see that my representations would be useless.' The wily Abbé had noticed that the actors were always quarrelling, that money was hard to come by, that his nephew was starting to find it all too much, and now his uncle was planning *le grand coup*; but he did not explain what he had in mind. Then he came to the point: '. . . this would already have been done if his wife was ready to act in concert with me and if she had less indulgence for her husband's fantasies'. This was of course Renée-Pélagie's problem: she was so constantly permissive that the Marquis assumed he was free to do anything he chose; she would never complain.

He had done as he wished in Paris but he had kept his '*phrenesies*' outside the marital apartments, which were located in or adjacent to his in-laws' residence. Now he was living in his own home and he assumed he could behave as he wished. If his passion for the theatre absorbed him, it was still not quite enough for a man who had been used to two very different aspects of personal life: either he fell romantically and desperately in love with out-of-reach aristocrats, actresses and courtesans or else he sought out working-class women and paid them for partnership in violent and/or unnatural sex. So what now? The seigneur of La Coste could not easily choose a mistress from neighbouring families, for then he would have lost the respect of his villagers, which he needed. It was the acting which gave him opportunities, and his wife was presumably too occupied with her children and too forgiving generally to notice what he felt about one actress in particular. He had already written about how one of his own theatrical heroes intended to use the heroine in his plays, 'for he understood clearly that through this he would gain the possibility of speaking to her about love'. Perhaps he wanted to do the same.

It will never be known if Renée-Pélagie noticed at this juncture that her husband was attracted by her sister, or attracted for the second time, if the story of his early fascination with the twelve-year-old girl is true. Neither will it be known at what point Anne-Prospère responded. Perhaps she hesitated. He was planning to take her with him on one of his many trips to Mazan to supervise the building work there, and he wrote to his steward François Ripert in February 1772: 'We shall arrive for supper, my sister-in-law, myself, a maid and a lackey.' Apparently he was not bringing his wife. Then very soon afterwards he wrote again to say that he would come alone, with one friend. There would be *point de dame*, no lady.

Perhaps Anne-Prospère had decided it was not politic to travel with the Marquis. There is no evidence that Renée-Pélagie went with him on these trips to Mazan but it is understandable that la Présidente, still over four hundred miles away in Paris, complained she had no news and that her young people were *très ambulants*, they moved about a good deal. It is only too evident that she was not invited to La Coste.

She told the Abbé that her daughter was deserving of pity for the way she accepted everything and although she, la Présidente, would arrange to pay some debts, in order to rescue the young people from dire trouble, she needed time. She continued to flatter the Abbé: if he approved with his presence this 'ridiculous and daily expenditure, it is in order to make it look honourable and to be of assistance to Madame your niece'.

La Présidente seemed to have had some foreboding of dire events, unless she was thinking only of money: 'I confess that if I did not know you to be near her I should die of anxiety.' Did she already have reliable spies or agents in the area? How much did she know? And how much did Renée-Pélagie know so far about her husband's writing? She knew he read a great deal, and he had a wide-ranging library at the château, while she herself does not seem to have read anything except the gazettes, for the time being. But he would certainly not have given her to read the much-quoted *Portrait de Julie* which he preserved, as though planning to include it in some future fiction. 'Julie' is assumed to have been Anne-Prospère, and this description reads like the picture of his ideal woman: she had attained 'the fortunate age when one begins to feel that the heart is made for loving; her attractive eyes announce this through their expression of the most tender voluptuousness; in her an interesting pallor is the image of desire. . . . Her mouth is small and pleasing; the delicate breeze of the zephyr is less pure than her breath'. She was tall and elegant, with a noble bearing and a graceful walk. 'Her character was equally charming, so was her mind. She learnt at an early age to listen to her own reason, dispensing in a philosophical manner with all the prejudices of education and childhood, she learnt to understand and make judgements at the age when others hardly know how to think.'

Sade's Julie was no submissive Sophie, as created by Rousseau, she was something of an intellectual, a liberated young woman, because she thought for herself: she realized that she was being encouraged to suppress natural emotions, by considering them as crimes, but she was not taken in and the writer dares to hope that she might be able to love him. Sade's manner is literary in the contemporary mode yet emotional, while his choice of the name 'Julie' could be meaningful. He and Anne-Prospère had surely both read *La nouvelle Héloïse*, published by Rousseau with huge success in 1761. It caused tears to be shed all over Europe and was known at the time as 'Julie', the name of its heroine. In his own novel *Aline et Valcour* (1795)

Sade was to write admiringly of Rousseau and even said that he had met him. The heroine of *La nouvelle Héloïse* was also a long way from Sophie, so predictably hated by Mary Wollstonecraft. She was the pre-romantic heroine *par excellence*, she could have been ready to follow 'nature', but like the earlier heroines of Corneille, Madeleine de Scudéry or Madame de Lafayette, she knew where her duty lay, she overcame her feelings and accepted an arranged marriage.

There was another aspect to the situation: Rousseau's heroine was an aristocrat; her family would not allow her to marry her tutor, Saint-Preux, who was a bourgeois. Sade the young aristocrat had wanted to marry another aristocrat, Laure de Lauris, he had apparently wanted to marry the beautiful Anne-Prospère when she was too young, and now he had been married for nine years to a plain, non-intellectual, non-aristocratic, virtuous woman who had money and loved him in an unchallenging way. He could have seen her as useful but dull. Sade, living as usual in an unreal world, saw Anne-Prospère, who was said to have fair hair and blue eyes, as the perfect partner, especially since, if she really was Julie, she was ready to reject convention. There were two other aspects to her attraction for him: his previous 'crimes' had both contained an element of impiety, of anti-religion, and now here was a girl who had presumably at least considered that one day she might become the Bride of Christ, a nun. And if these two became lovers, would they be committing something like incest? It is worth remembering that the theme of incest was to preoccupy Sade in much of his fiction, notably in *Eugénie de Franval*, *Dorgeville*, *Florville et Courval*, even in *Aline et Valcour*. The theme of *La Comtesse de Sancerre*, in which a mother tries to kill her daughter's fiancé, was to have a different kind of relevance later.

The relationship between Sade and Anne-Prospère, however obscure, was more than a biographical rumour but came to light, presumably shattering Renée-Pélagie, only through her husband's next bout of unpredictable behaviour. It has been suggested that his sister-in-law had refused his advances until he was exasperated, causing him to break away from the château and even from his beloved theatre in search of sexual excitement and satisfaction, to be achieved as in the past through violence. It was unpredictable but typical in its way, particularly because Sade's clumsiness led to the whole plan going wrong. Something, in the third week of June 1772, caused him to travel the sixty miles or so to Marseille, accompanied by his valet Latour, and spend several hours with a group of prostitutes whom he had hoped to stimulate into sessions of flagellation and sodomy with an aphrodisiac much used at the time, sweets or pastilles laced with Spanish fly. He had gone to Marseille, between the presentation of two plays at La Coste, ostensibly to cash a *lettre de change*, and returned two days later as though nothing had happened. But it had, the pastilles had been overdosed with cantharides, the Spanish fly, and two girls were so ill they thought they were dying.

They didn't die, but they complained, and by 11 July four men arrived at La Coste: the bailiff from Apt, escorted by a sergeant and four mounted constables. They had come to arrest Sade and Latour, who were accused of poisoning and sodomy. But the accused men were not there. Neither was Madame de Sade, nor her sister. The only person in authority they could talk to was the lawyer, Antoine Fage. He said that the two accused persons had not been seen for a week and there had been no news of them. What had happened to Renée-Pélagie and her sister? Where had they gone? The Marquise had presumably been told at least something of what had happened, and her reaction is not hard to imagine. Her husband had already decided to make his escape, taking Latour with him. It was thought by early biographers that he had also taken Anne-Prospère with him, but this has since been discounted. The proof is that she helped her elder sister in the first and obvious step that had to be taken: Renée-Pélagie, following the precedent of the Rose Keller case, decided that she must go to Marseille and buy off the girls, hoping they would withdraw their accusations. It was six years since the Arcueil scandal, and it had been la Présidente who had produced the money in the attempt to silence Rose Keller. Now Renée-Pélagie had to proceed on her own, for an appeal to her mother was flatly refused. La Présidente had been horrified when she heard about the relationship between her son-in-law and her younger daughter, but it is not clear how and when she heard, for did even Renée-Pélagie know? More importantly in one way she had not reckoned with the fact that her eldest daughter was now quite grown up.

Fortunately Anne-Prospère, who must still have been on good terms with Renée, presumably down-playing or explaining her relationship with Sade, agreed to go to Marseille with her sister, and equally fortunately Ripert was able to produce the necessary money. All the same this cannot have been an easy or pleasant trip for the two young women, especially for the wife who had hoped against hope that her husband would never involve her again in this sort of situation.

If the girls in Marseille were bought off, the judiciary, aware of the Rose Keller case, were not going to let the matter drop. A second trip to Marseille by the indefatigable Marquise did not influence the magistrates and she realized with horror just how dangerous the situation was. Her husband and his valet had gone into hiding and she had no idea where they were. It was believed by romantic interpreters of the story that Anne-Prospère had gone with the two men, but if this has been disproved she certainly followed them. She was still at La Coste when the two young women received an unexpected visitor: their father. Madame de Montreuil, *maîtresse femme* though she was, had no doubt decided that a masculine presence at the château was now essential, especially that of an experienced legal man, even if he was now retired and still an object of possible revenge by supporters of Chancellor Maupéou. Were the sisters on speaking terms? It is not clear, but Anne-Prospère's relationship with her brother-in-law was known in Paris, and her mother's fulminations became melodramatic and intense. The Président gave his elder daughter some useful money and surely made it clear to her that at last somebody in her own family was standing by her.

But what was to be done about the verdict of the Marseille court? Sade was convicted of poisoning and sodomy, his valet Latour of sodomy only, and the sentence was confirmed on 11 September by the Parlement de Provence at Aix. The sentence was harsh: public confession, fines and then death. This was to be carried out on the class-conscious terms current at the time: decapitation for the Marquis, hanging or strangulation for Latour, after which their bodies would be incinerated. Since the culprits were convicted *in absentia*, they were burnt only in effigy.

If Renée-Pélagie did not know it, her father would certainly tell her, that this sentence would remain in effect for thirty years – a lifetime. If her husband chose to appear in court to answer the charges against him, he must do so within the next five years.

As though this threat was not terrifying enough, Renée-Pélagie now found herself entirely alone. Her father, having made a few potentially useful visits among legal advisers and the judiciary, returned to Paris, not before, apparently, expressing admiration for Gothon and her beautiful bottom. This was the only amusing anecdote surviving from his visit, which was deeply overshadowed by something else: Renée-Pélagie's sister had left the château in order to join Sade on a kind of illicit honeymoon in Italy.

This story, naturally enough, preoccupied romantic writers of the nineteenth century, while all researchers and biographers who followed them have attempted to prove what did or did not happen. It is now accepted that Anne-Prospère did travel with her brother-in-law, who on the journey called himself the Comte de Mazan, to Venice and other cities and that she travelled as his wife. Sade himself referred to the interlude much later. The other known fact is that she did not travel for very long, for on 2 October she was back at La Coste. Why this so-called 'honeymoon' did not last longer is a tempting subject for speculation. Did the couple quarrel? Was there a failure in love or sex? Did Anne-Prospère feel guilty? Or was she sent by the 'criminal' on the run to find out what was happening in France? There had been one significant development from Renée-Pélagie's point of view: whatever she felt about her husband's behaviour, she had to accept that he had now lost his civil rights, and after a *conseil de famille* in September she had been appointed administrator of his affairs, especially in relation to the children. She had predictably refused any question of a *séparation de biens*.

Chronology is difficult at this point in 1772 when the story enters its cloak-and-dagger phase and becomes a *vie romancée*, a historical romance, except that it is not a romance, it is true. Anne-Prospère had come back from Italy in early October and was once thought to have joined the Marquis a second time. It is now known, however, that the two sisters were in Paris in October, after a Montreuil relative had taken them there. Was Renée-Pélagie as understanding and forgiving of her sister as she was of her husband?

If the two young women established some sort of *modus vivendi*, as they surely did, their mother was having none of it. The mere fact that Anne-Prospère had travelled to Italy with her brother-in-law, accompanied only by the valet Latour, who after all had been convicted at Marseille with his master, was enough to destroy her reputation. How could a daughter of hers, a canoness, do such a thing? And supposing she returned to secular life, which implied married life, who would marry her now? Madame de Montreuil, acutely aware of this problem, no doubt felt she deserved better luck with her next arranged marriage, for her attempt to ally her elder daughter with an old-established family of the *noblesse d'épée* had gone wrong. However, she was not one to feel any guilt. She blamed Renée-Pélagie's forgiving nature, which she saw as weakness, something she could tolerate only if it suited her own plans. She failed entirely to understand the extraordinary, indefinable bond that held Renée and her husband together, which had no place in conventional life as she saw it. And the unthinkable had happened: Anne-Prospère was in revolt too.

La Présidente had two objectives now: Sade must be found, if only to appeal against the Aix conviction, which indeed was based on questionable evidence in the end; and as for Anne-Prospère, there must be an immediate search for any incriminating documents, letters from either party and any relevant manuscripts by the Marquis, who liked to keep copies of his most passionate outpourings.

Renée-Pélagie knew her husband was outside France, but the notes from him she received through Fage did not satisfy her. She wanted him back, if he could come back safely, and he must have been keen to come back too, for he left Italy and went to Chambéry, not in France at the time but the capital of Savoy, itself part of the kingdom of Sardinia. Sade had not lost the naïveté that accompanied his gift for lying and his insistence on living out the unreal, the theatrical, in preference to the practical. He wrote to his mother-in-law and told her where he was, apparently convinced that there was hope of his conviction being quashed. Perhaps he hoped she would merely pay the right money to the right people. She replied at once, but not by letter. She had never lost her contacts with influential people and by 8 December, after she had put her case neatly to the French ambassador to Sardinia, her son-in-law was arrested at the house he had rented near Chambéry, relieved of his sword and two pistols and taken to the prison known as the Bastille of the Dukes of Savoy – the hilltop Château de Miolans, about fourteen miles from Chambéry.

Of Anne-Prospère there was no sign, although a woman had been seen at the Chambéry house, and it is known that the Marquis had arranged for her baggage, with his own, to be deposited in Nice.

The Marquis naturally pleaded for his release, writing rather feebly to the Governor of Savoy that he had committed no crime against France, he had done nothing to offend the civil or criminal law, and adding that his wife wanted him back. He suspected rightly that his mother-in-law had arranged his imprisonment and he knew why. The cause was a possible marriage for Anne-Prospère, for her parents were apparently considering an offer on behalf of the Vicomte de Beaumont, one of the nephews of the Archbishop of Paris. Unfortunately

this powerful uncle was a known reactionary, ready to con-
demn any form of unconventional behaviour, and la Présidente,
knowing this, became desperate in her attempts to find any of
those dangerous documents which might mention or implicate
Anne-Prospère. In addition to her search for papers, which she
thought to be contained in a little red chest, she wanted to
know if anyone had found any clothing not belonging to the
Marquis, fearing Anne-Prospère might have left some behind.
She had also been dismayed to hear that Sade, before his imprisonment, had been ill, and she wanted details. She was terrified that he might have been suffering from some venereal
disease. If so, and if he had been Anne-Prospère's lover, then
she would have contracted it too. These inquiries led nowhere,
but the Beaumont family made their conditions cruelly plain:
the Marquis must be locked up for life, otherwise no marriage. And there was none.

In the meantime Renée-Pélagie developed further than ever
her active role in the freeing of her husband. She thought of
nothing else. Her mother probably did not realize how active
she would become, how far she too would enter into the melodrama. She left Paris late in February 1773, alleging that she
must return to La Coste, for in any case her children had remained there. Early in March, however, she wrote to the
Governor of Savoy that her plans to see her husband had been
held up by her own bad health: '. . . a heavy cold has stopped
me at Barraux' – about twelve miles from Chambéry. She was
very worried, for she had had no news of her husband for
over a month. She was planning a new move, and perhaps she
had learnt from the plays she had seen and acted in at La
Coste, perhaps acting could be useful as well as romantic and
entertaining. She decided to appear in the area not as Madame
de Sade but dressed as a man. She was now a 'Monsieur Dumont',
and she came not alone but accompanied by her 'brother'.
How had she recruited him? He was named Albaret and he
had once worked for Sade. This strange couple maintained they
were traders on their way to Piedmont. This second 'Monsieur
Dumont' was later in the pay of the Montreuils. Now, however,

he came to the prison, hoping to see the Marquis, but he was rebuffed, succeeding only in delivering a letter from the Marquise to her husband.

Renée stayed at a not too reputable inn at Montmélian, some four miles from the prison, and either from there or soon afterwards she continued to write pleading letters on her husband's behalf, saying to the King of Sardinia, for example, that he was no villain: 'An over-lively imagination has produced, Sire, a kind of offence: punishment has made it into a crime, justice has released its thunderbolts. And why? for a youthful excess which attacked neither the life, nor the honour, nor the reputation of citizens.' She maintained that a stay at Miolans would not 'calm the fire of an over-lively imagination', it would make it worse.

Nobody could have agreed with her, except of course the prisoner, and he had plenty of time to use that imagination. He chose to continue his acting, he pretended to behave well. He even took communion at Easter, and during the night of 30 April 1773 he made a clever escape, together with another difficult prisoner. He left two letters for the authorities, indicating that he had received valuable help from his wife: 'I have the advantage in my escape of help which my wife is sending from my property. This help consists of fifteen men, well mounted, well armed, who are waiting for me below the château.' There were of course no such men, but all these colourful details at least provide some additional reasons why Renée-Pélagie was so devoted to him: he was such a convincing showman. And he revealed more of this talent in the letters which he left to be read after his escape, asking for his effects to be sent on to his wife and reminding the staff to look after the two young setter dogs he had been allowed to have. He was sorry to have caused the governor so much trouble, for he had been honest and kind to him. As Sade and his companion continued their escape, by way of Grenoble, he wrote one last note to the governor, in grand heroic terms: he preferred death to the loss of his liberty.

4 *Permissive Partner*

Are you sure they [novels] are all horrid? – Catherine
Morland in *Northanger Abbey*

On 10 May 1773 Renée-Pélagie was probably telling a lie
– she had learnt the technique by now – when she told the
Governor of Savoy that her husband, the escaped prisoner,
had indeed come to La Coste but had stayed there for twenty-
four hours only, having then left again for 'a place unknown
to his persecutors'. Those who have followed the Sade for-
tunes know only that he spent some time in Bordeaux and
may then have been to Spain, possibly Cadiz, but the evidence
is not convincing. He had in fact written to his mother-in-law,
hoping that she might finance his journey, for in that way he
could safely stay outside French territory. But she refused his
request, since she now definitely wanted him in prison. Once
there he would have the chance to appeal against the Aix judgement which had been made in his absence. His wife wanted
him free and with her at La Coste. In the meantime he needed
money, and it was Renée-Pélagie who had to search out a
money-lender in order to help him.

Between mother and daughter the rift was widening fast,
mainly because la Présidente was becoming obsessed by her
search for those dangerous papers which might incriminate her
younger daughter. Although she had at first raised no objection

when the Marquise tried to obtain her husband's effects from Miolans, she soon decided to apply for them herself, for she had heard they included papers. She arranged for them all to be placed in one room and then had the room sealed – the prison governor obeyed all her commands. In this way she prevented the recovery of these accumulated clothes and objects by her daughter, who made the journey to Miolans to claim them and was forced to leave empty-handed. Sade himself stated that there were no papers among the odd collection of things he had left behind.

Renée-Pélagie grew more frustrated every day because her mother seemed to be winning this long-running battle. She did not realize that it had hardly begun. Could there have been any dangerous papers at the château? Perhaps the vindictive lady in Paris had been informed by the autumn that the 'author' had secretly returned to his estates, and perhaps he and his papers could be found there? In the meantime he had indeed returned, despite the danger of arrest, for he felt safe there, mainly because he truly loved La Coste and surely also because Renée-Pélagie was there to answer any inquiries or deal with creditors or search-parties. She was, after all, a 'respectable lady', as the lawyer Antoine Fage described her, and both husband and wife were convinced they could trust their staff. Only one person close to the family had, they eventually decided, let them down. This was Fage himself, who understood and liked Renée-Pélagie, but he knew she would never hear one word against her husband. By now the hard-pressed lawyer could no longer cope with the impatient creditors who surrounded the ménage, and he was upset by the Marquis's threats of physical violence against him when no money could be found. Inevitably, if regretfully, Fage moved closer to Madame de Montreuil. He felt he could trust her in one way, for eventually, he was convinced, she would pay at least some of the bills, including even his own. He was undecided for a time, he felt he had a duty to the family and he worried about Madame de Sade. What might happen to her? He thought he had noticed some improvement in her husband, who seemed now 'constant' in his behaviour towards her and might even remain 'calm' for some time.

In the end, after the Sades noticed some irregularities in his conduct of business and were also aware of his new relationship with Madame de Montreuil, he was replaced, early in 1774, by the notary Gaspard Gaufridy of Apt, who had known Sade when they had both been schoolboys in Provence. But in the meantime there had been a night of melodrama at the château. Fage had known it was being planned, he had even been involved, although he had advised against it. The plans had been formed at the end of 1773, for on 16 December the King himself had issued an order to the Lieutenant-General of Police: any papers for which Sade was responsible must be seized, Sade must be arrested and taken to Pierre-Encise near Lyon, where he had been detained following the Rose Keller incident in 1768. The original *lettre de cachet* was still in force. Sade's publisher and biographer Jean-Jacques Pauvert has suggested that the 'author' was suspected of producing not only letters and documents likely to destroy the honour of his wife's family and his own, but he may have embarked on potentially seditious writing as Beaumarchais had done in his highly successful *Mémoires*, published just at this time. The King and his ministers were having no more of that, and such an attitude was certainly helpful to Madame de Montreuil, who had been at least partly responsible for the issuing of the royal order, concentrating on her son-in-law's treatment of her two daughters and, by implication, the dishonouring of her own grandchildren.

Sadly, at the receiving end of all this secret and despotic activity was one woman in a Provençal village: Renée-Pélagie de Sade. Just before 6 January 1774 her husband had received a warning from some trustworthy person, possibly Ripert, and had left the château. Every night the drawbridge was raised, but that did not deter the party of men, led by a police inspector from Paris and escorted by mounted constabulary, who appeared outside the walls during the hours of darkness. The chatelaine herself was asleep at the time and her awakening was rough: 'Ladders were put in place, the château walls were scaled, the men entered, pistols and swords in their hands.' Renée-Pélagie, who later signed this graphic account, appeared and was confronted by the officer in charge. 'With the fury caused by his action displayed on his face he asked her, with dreadful oaths and the most indecent expressions, where was Monsieur de Sade, her husband, he was wanted dead or alive?' Signing this statement later with a detailed description of the invasion, and describing herself as 'the petitioner', Renée-Pélagie referred to the cruelty of the situation. 'She saw barbarity before her eyes; horror and terror racked her in succession: she saw the work of her mother, she could not conceal the fact from herself.'

In her statement Renée-Pélagie referred to the respect she still felt for her mother, her rank and her sex, despite the insults to which she herself was now subjected. She then described how she replied to the officer's question, honestly, that 'her husband was not there'. This led the invaders to the most violent action. They split into two groups: part of them were sent out to guard the avenues to the château, the rest prepared to break down doors and smash furniture. Acting no doubt on precise orders from Paris, but adding violence of their own, the raiders entered the Marquis's study, tore down family portraits from the walls, broke open the cabinets, seized all the documents they found and burnt some on the orders of their leader, who then took away others, 'without giving the petitioner the slightest indication of what they contained'.

Even worse was to come. Papers were snatched from Renée-Pélagie's hands, and so was the tortoise-shell snuff-box she had apparently picked up. It was decorated with gold and the lid carried a miniature portrait. Could it have been a portrait of her husband? What would happen to him? Would she ever see him again? The men insisted that they were only carrying out the orders of 'la Dame de Montreuil', and they uttered one final barbaric threat – they had been ordered to fire three pistol-shots each at the Marquis de Sade and take his dead body to la Dame. It was not true, but it was meant to be a serious warning. Somehow Renée-Pélagie wrote a three-line note, in her most picturesque spelling, probably to Ripert, telling him urgently to keep Sade away, and adding: 'Come at once, don't delay one minute.'

Maître Fage, who had not yet been dismissed by the family, went to comfort the Marquise the next day – perhaps he was feeling guilty – and told her mother that he would not have left her alone, but fortunately someone was with her, a Sieur de Vaux from Montélimar. Renée-Pélagie must have been deeply upset by this incident, as would any woman on discovering that her own mother had directed such an operation against her own husband. Evidently, everything had got out of hand and it was she herself who had suffered most.

She had no reason to doubt what the police officer had told her and she now decided how best to carry out a twofold plan, to save her husband and defeat her mother. There was only one thing to do: she must lodge an official complaint against la Présidente, in accordance with conventional legal procedure, as her husband had already advised her, and she must go to Paris to follow up any method, conventional or not, which would help free him. Although he had very few friends, he had not chosen the life of a solitary wanderer – he told François Ripert that he did not enjoy it, he was not made for that. And as for Renée-Pélagie, against all odds and, it might seem, against all common sense, she loved the man, she wanted him with her.

Some four to six weeks after the failed raid on La Coste the Marquis wrote optimistically to Ripert saying he must disappear briefly, since Madame de Montreuil had promised to sort out all the problems, civil and criminal. He offered sureties for the money he now needed, arranged a secret stay with Ripert at Mazan and then added instructions involving his wife: she would also stay for a week with him, but she was not going to arrive secretly under cover of darkness, as he was going to do: '... arriving by day and in public she will not be able to be there incognito, but as soon as she arrives, my dear Ripert, you will be kind enough to call on all the ladies of the town to give them greetings on Madame's behalf, and tell them how very sorry she is that her situation and the amount of business she has to transact (the only reason for her trip) deprive her of the pleasure of going to see them and of receiving them at your house'. Then Ripert's doors were to be hermetically sealed and the Sades would see only him and his family. The Marquis gave instructions as to how the steward would help arrange his own getaway, after which Madame must be taken back to La Coste in a mule-drawn carriage. Would Ripert please escort her, for she would be alone. Money was needed and would be raised by a variety of means, from land transfers to the pawning of silver and promises of money from Madame. Then Sade left for Italy.

His wife was left with a double financial problem: she had to raise money to support him in Italy and somehow she had to keep the château going. She did not usually send the housekeeper Gothon out to collect food and household goods, for there was little transport and no money with which to pay for anything. She sent lists to Ripert which show that she was at least trying to keep up standards. When she ordered thirty bottles of wine she specified 'the best', but when after ordering 'a few plump chickens, a turkey, a hare' she asked for partridges, they should be bought only if not too expensive. Remembering her husband's interest in the estate, and thinking of the future, she also ordered two hundred young cherry trees, ready for planting. She had to list what she could offer in return for all these services, including the money to be sent to her husband in Italy, and it is sad to learn that a silver-gilt platter and also a silver coffee-pot could go. If more was wanted, then she also had a jewel box or a silver medallion.

It was she who was left to cope with the creditors, including 'the Jew Beaucaire' who happened to come to La Coste when she was not there. In order to take his revenge on the penniless seigneurial ménage, he caused a scene in the château and also outside in the village.

The chatelaine could not hope for any protection from gossip.

Renée-Pélagie's plight could not be kept secret and it was symptomatic of the state of France in the 1770s, for the aristocracy had neglected their estates, leaving the management to others whom they failed to supervise. When the British agriculturist Arthur Young had visited France earlier he had noticed this situation. The successful and more prudent middle-class families had been buying land, especially near Paris and the other cities. They had every intention of managing their estates with more competence than those who had inherited land over the centuries and never questioned their rights.

The Sades were far from alone in their system of living on credit. All their class did so, it was the accepted method, but they took it to excess. An entrapped and poverty-stricken wife, as Renée-Pélagie was now, cuts a sad figure, far from rare in the history of married women's problems, and the domestic details which were recorded, mainly by herself, provide a depressing commentary on the way she lived. However, she had chosen to live this way, she had refused the *séparation de biens*, and if nothing would change her attitude, she herself had changed, inevitably. After eleven years of marriage what remained of the well-brought-up girl who had seen nothing outside her parents' comfortable residences and possibly a convent? How far had her love for her husband been conditioned by her inevitable revolt against her authoritarian mother? As things stood between herself and 'la Dame de Montreuil' it looked as though she had inherited no useful characteristics from that strong-minded lady. Had Renée-Pélagie made any effort, however indirect, to counteract her husband's apparently incorrigible excesses, or had she given up at the first attempt, if there had ever been one? Perhaps she had tried to curb his behaviour by her own example, but for her example always meant understanding, acceptance, forgiveness and the practical attempts to solve problems, especially financial ones. Was her reaction due to love, fear or the realization that she could never change her husband? Did she even seriously want to? Years later he was to write that he would not change, and he didn't, she was the one who changed, otherwise she would surely have had to

leave him. Her arranged marriage, arranged to satisfy the social
ambitions of her family and the financial needs of the Sades,
had produced three children but otherwise only negative results: neither she nor her husband had any ready money for
the ever-spiralling debts, she was forced to pawn and borrow,
and instead of the splendid social life her mother had antici-
pated for her she was now virtually a prisoner with few friends
(hardly any names from this period have been preserved), and
relying for help on a small group of professional men and
servants whom she could not pay. Thankfully her mother had
taken responsibility for the children. She herself seems to have
had no ambitions; she had merely accepted what her family
had planned for her. In his future writings her husband fre-
quently attacked the system of arranged marriages, but Renée-
Pélagie for the time being had no complaint against the custom.
Where was the alternative? She would have had to live at home
with the mother who was known to prefer her sister or she
would have had to live like that sister – in a convent or simi-
lar religious establishment. As it was, she had reached a state
of social degradation because she preferred the man she loved
– and if she treated him in some ways like a difficult child she
may have realized, if she had seen any of his writings, or if he
had talked to her about them, that he was a man apart. She
had seen him directing plays, she had taken part in them and
perhaps she regarded her impossibly difficult life as a new act
or scene, the sequel to all that had taken place in that *salle de
comédie*, now presumably deserted.

At the same time she unconsciously regarded herself as co-
author, with her husband, of the play they were living out
together. This woman of thirty-three seemed to symbolize something
of the new and uneasy relationship between the old aristocracy
and the constantly rising professional middle classes. The Sades
and the Montreuils could have merged, so to speak, Renée-
Pélagie might have spent part of her life close to court circles,
or even in the salons, but instead she had learnt to live in a
way for which she had not been destined, apparently condo-
ning sexual excess and perversion, seeing them as no more

than a sinister form of current *galanterie*, and living dangerously, between visits from creditors, on more and more borrowed money. She experienced all that was worst, and nothing
that was potentially best, about the *ancien régime*.

If the theatre was deserted, however, the château was not,
and family life, the strange family life which Renée-Pélagie had
come to accept, was far from over, for in June that year Anne-
Prospère came to stay and Sade himself returned from Italy. If
these two latter had been lovers, any such illicit romance was
now over, and in Paris the political climate had changed, for
in May King Louis XV had died from smallpox. His surviving
grandson, now Louis XVI, was inexperienced and known to
be prudish, unlike his father. His officials decided not to shock
him by communicating police files about libertine behaviour,
but very soon important administrative changes were planned.
By August 1774 the unpopular Chancellor Maupéou was dismissed and the Parlements, which he had attempted to suppress,
were to be restored. Renée-Pélagie realized that this would help
her husband and looked forward to the time when he would
be allowed to appeal against the 1772 condemnation at Aix-
en-Provence. In any case, the charge of poisoning would certainly be dropped, for the two girls involved had withdrawn
their complaints and had now completely recovered. In the
meantime, however, Sade did not stay long at La Coste because
legally he could still be detained under the original *lettre de
cachet* which had confined him to Miolans. It could have been
automatically cancelled after the death of the King, but Madame
de Montreuil, knowing that, had immediately renewed it.

Renée-Pélagie and Anne-Prospère, apparently now on good
sisterly terms, went to Paris in July in the hope that Renée
could pursue the case against Madame de Montreuil. If Renée-
Pélagie could defeat her mother, then this mother would be in
a weak position in her attempts to have Sade imprisoned.

There was some hope for him, because if Madame de
Montreuil was behaving 'like a lioness', as her daughter wrote,
she was still not always logical in the way she went about
things, and would not always achieve the results she wanted.

The petition which had been submitted earlier in the year to the important royal court, the Châtelet, had been skilfully drafted by Sade, who obviously saw it all in theatrical terms, and then signed by his wife. If some of it was now ancient history, it presents a fascinating picture of how the Sade–Anne-Prospère situation had developed, how the Marseille affair had been glossed over and how far, allegedly, 'la Dame de Montreuil' had taken her enmity towards her son-in-law. Her sister, said the Marquise, had come to La Coste 'on the pretext of keeping her company and enjoying a calmer atmosphere' and in 'the peace and quiet that nothing should have disturbed' nothing led her to suspect the 'fatal passion' that caused so much trouble. The petitioner then referred to her husband's visit to Marseille, after which she heard that he was being charged with some offence he had allegedly committed in that town. 'She turned to her sister, but the disturbance she noted in her state of mind, the confused nature of her replies only added to her agitation.' It looks as though Sade may have confided in Anne-Prospère but not in his wife – understandably, perhaps.

But if that episode was over, Madame de Montreuil's anger was not. She must have been exceptionally angry after that raid on the château, for everything had gone wrong: she had forbidden any violence, but it had happened, no papers were found and the whole thing was so expensive that even la Présidente was temporarily in difficulties. Now, however, her daughter was in difficulties, because no action had been taken following her petition, and since she was not on speaking terms with her mother that summer, she did not stay with her but at a hotel in the rue Taranne, which was in the Faubourg Saint-Germain. She was sure her mother was spying on her and she asked Gaufridy in Apt to send any letters to a tailor named Carlier in the rue Saint-Nicaise. (Later this same tailor made many clothes for her husband.) She had gained enough confidence by now to see Monsieur Chapote, the royal prosecutor, and liked him, finding him young, intelligent and kind. However, he quietly decided to do nothing about this seemingly difficult case. Perhaps Madame de Montreuil had taken a hand, through bribery or other means. In any case Chapote spread an unkind rumour: the Marquise, he said, was mad. If she did not hear about this she heard something else. She was told, and in turn she told Gaufridy, that her mother was 'madly in love with M. de Sade and that she was much angrier with me than with him'. The gossips would not know of course how in the early years of the Sade marriage Madame de Montreuil had referred to her son-in-law as *le drôle d'enfant* and maybe only his mother-in-law knew that in 1765 or 1766 he had once written *ma chère maman* in a letter to her, probably his usual way of addressing her at the time. If he had once been her 'child' he had soon become a more than rebellious adolescent, but these two strong characters were inevitably attracted to one another, even in hostility; they challenged each other, they enjoyed the fight.

Renée-Pélagie's reaction to this gossip was ironic: '*tant mieux*', she said, things could hardly be worse. She was disillusioned with Chapote, who uttered 'sophisms' in order to calm her, and she preferred Sartine, the Lieutenant-General of Police. She thought he was more practical. In the end nobody did anything but she herself heard more about the attitude of the Beaumont family towards a possible marriage for her sister: the idea that the marriage would take place only if Sade were imprisoned for life struck her as *indigne*, unworthy, shameful. However, Renée-Pélagie and everyone else could be glad of one thing: Sade's appeal against the Aix judgement, she was told, would eventually be heard that autumn and she thought it would be safer and much cheaper for him to come back to La Coste now. She left Paris, he left Italy and they met in Lyon.

The curtain went up on a new act. In the second act of his play about Renée-Pélagie's life the late Yukio Mishima attempted to imagine what has remained unimaginable, the so-called orgies, the mysterious and disturbing scenes that took place at La Coste during the late autumn and winter of 1774/5.

MADAME DE MONTREUIL: ... The five women and the man, all stark naked, were desperately running this way and that, trying to escape his whip, imploring his pardon. The long black whip darted about the room, like a swallow under the eaves of the château. And you ...

RENÉE: Ahh — (*Covers her face.*)

MADAME DE MONTREUIL: ... were hanging by your hands from the chandelier, naked. Drops of blood, like raindrops coursing down a forsythia stem in the rain, shone on your body in the firelight, as you dangled, half-unconscious with pain. ...

La Présidente, in the play, maintains that her agent saw this scene, and its horrifying sequel, as he stood concealed on a balcony outside one of the windows. Mishima transmuted reports on what might have happened, adding lurid colours of his own, into a scene from a Sade novel, and the details of what is known to have happened belong to the Marquis's biography. But how closely was Renée-Pélagie involved and what motivated her behaviour? Possibly she was frightened, for the estrangement from her mother had left her desperately alone. Possibly too she was still hoping against hope that she could somehow rehabilitate her husband by helping him indulge his fantasies. When in the past he had gone out looking for prostitutes she could not go with him, but if his 'victims' could be brought into the château, she herself would be on hand to prevent harmful excess – and surely the police could not follow.

This new act had begun in Lyon, where the Marquis engaged a group of young 'servants', found for him by a young woman whom he later described as a 'procuress', Anne Sablonnière, or 'Nanon'. How could his wife encourage him to do this, when there were already servants at La Coste and hardly any money to pay them with? Either she was terrorized or she was indeed 'mad', as the Paris prosecutor had described her. Had she even identified with her husband, as Mishima and others have maintained? There is no easy answer, not even the suggestion that she was deepening the rebellion against her authoritarian mother or her own excuse that she was dismissing all the former servants and needed people now who had never heard of the trouble in Marseille in 1772.

They would have been difficult to find. In addition, la Présidente was not only well informed through mysterious people she no doubt paid handsomely, but she knew her daughter and had realized what was happening, although she could not pretend to understand it. When she stated that the Marquise wrote only what was dictated to her she was probably right, for this submissive attitude was not limited to letters and continued in Lyon. Her husband wanted to employ a young man named André as a secretary but his parents wanted references. It was the Marquise who approached Gaufridy: 'You will receive a letter,' she wrote, 'in which you will be asked if Monsieur le Comte de Mazan, at present in Lyon, is the same person as the Marquis de Sade who was tried at Aix.' (The Marquis used the former name when attempting to conceal his identity, as when he had travelled with Anne-Prospère). She asked the lawyer to reply 'with a little lie in the Jesuitical style, which, without compromising you, confirms however that it is not the same man'. He was to refer to the other branches of the Sade family and indicate that the Sade who was tried at Aix was surely abroad and could not be the man who was now in Lyon. He was though undoubtedly the man who had inspired the letter, and the wife who had once been too pious for his taste had been ready to sign it. The boy André, as later became clear, could hardly spell, and he seemed destined to be a victim not a secretary.

There were not many men at La Coste. There was a valet called Jean, whom Renée-Pélagie found valuable, and Sade's own faithful valet La Jeunesse, who had abandoned his wife and children and was now living with Gothon. And then there was Nanon, who had gathered together five young girls of about fifteen and two older ones, in Lyon and Vienne. At the château she worked as a chambermaid and when Sade wanted to discredit her he called her a procuress. He also slept with her. Renée-Pélagie's health was obviously upset by the changed atmosphere of La Coste and she thought for a time that she was pregnant. A few months later she was convinced she wasn't, although Nanon was.

Sade did not write *Les 120 journées de Sodome* until 1782 or so, but understandably all biographers and critics have assumed that the author recalled, as he wrote it, something of his own château during that winter of 1774/5. La Coste was to grow in his imagination into the repellent Château de Silling, but if the four villains who conducted the orgies in the book were attempted projections of Sade's own self, at least there is no obvious portrait of Renée-Pélagie. Her portrait remains conjectural. In his play Mishima makes her cry out ecstatically that she *is* her husband: 'I am Alphonse!' She illustrates at this point of her career exactly what Simone de Beauvoir meant when she described *The Woman in Love*, in Part VI of *The Second Sex*: 'The supreme happiness of the woman in love is to be recognized by the loved man as a part of himself; when he says "we", she is associated and identified with him, she shares his prestige and reigns with him over the rest of the world. . . .' In this way Renée-Pélagie, in love with her 'Alphonse', as Mishima called him, reigned over the small, secret world of La Coste.

If in many ways Renée had changed, she still shared with her husband the astonishing naïveté which in his case had so often led him to invite calamity. Of course the victimized children escaped; of course their parents complained. How could this not have happened? News of the scandal soon spread, and just as soon it reached Madame de Montreuil. In any case her daughter, not knowing what to do, had written to her for advice. She at once made contact with Gaufridy and began to conduct operations: she was like some military commander who chose not to come to the battlefield, as though aware that she was too grand. The Abbé also received his orders but he refused to obey them. He was not going to Aix, as requested by Madame de Montreuil, in an attempt to influence the justices.

If Renée-Pélagie thought she had successfully broken away from her mother, she hadn't, which explains why she was reduced to asking her for advice. She and her husband were living so far outside reality that they had not foreseen what would happen. Predictably, the servant children's parents threatened to go to law, for some of the victims carried visible scars and bruises. How could the evidence of this 'really horrid' episode be suppressed? Madame de Montreuil said the girls must all be sent or taken back to their parents, but one girl had been so badly hurt that she was sent to the Abbé for safe keeping. He was desperately embarrassed and must have thought his niece a truly changed woman when she blackmailed him into keeping the girl. Did it cost Renée-Pélagie anything to sign a letter, obviously written by her husband, reminding the Abbé of his own sexual misdeeds? However, the trick worked. Another girl ran away to a convent and again Renée-Pélagie was revealed in a bad light. The prior wrote to the Abbé about this girl and said that the Marquise de Sade was no better than her husband. Worst sin of all, nobody at the château had taken their Easter communion that spring and the Marquise had allowed the girls to talk to a 'Lutheran', doubtless Gothon. He seemed to think she was married, but for the time being she was merely cohabiting with Sade's valet, La Jeunesse.

The once pious Renée-Pélagie was more than angry and she denied the accusations that she was the 'director of her husband's pleasures'. She was angry, on her mother's behalf in fact, that the Abbé had preserved his 'Stoic tranquillity'. His refusal to help his nephew justified everything that she and her husband thought about him. Her mother refused to accept her daughter's role as a ringleader and reminded Gaufridy that the abused girls had not complained about her: '... on the contrary. They speak of her as being compromised herself and the first victim of a fury that one can only see as madness'. She worried about her daughter and was afraid her life might be in danger. At the same time she knew that the young woman never once complained and that 'She would let herself be cut in pieces' rather than do anything that might harm her husband.

Probably the worst thing Renée-Pélagie ever did in her life was the way she got rid of Nanon. If she was unconcerned that this girl gave birth to the baby fathered, it was thought, by the Marquis, she was intent on silencing her accusations about her own treatment and that of the other girls. The Marquise herself actually buried some silver cutlery in the garden and accused Nanon of stealing it. In this way the girl could be removed from the château and nobody would believe her accusations. How could the woman who signed herself Montreuil de Sade do such a thing? But she did, and there were terrible scenes between the two women. Nanon was so hard to silence that it was decided to remove her from the convent to which she had fled by imprisoning her under a *lettre de cachet*. Madame de Montreuil duly obtained this and the poor girl spent two and a half years in prison at Arles. Nobody had dared tell her that her baby daughter had died, because the wet-nurse at La Coste was found to be pregnant herself and could not feed the infant. Nanon's father, who lived in the Auvergne, wrote a moving letter in 1777, inquiring what had happened to his daughter's baby and uttering a sentence that proved clearly what humble people were thinking: 'If such violent acts are permitted, we are no longer in France, where nobody is treated like a slave.'

Unfortunately, at the Château de La Coste, this is precisely what had happened. Fortunately for Nanon, who had made life very difficult for everyone, she eventually obtained work with a trader in Marseille, but Madame de Montreuil continued to have her watched. Sade himself, whose life was entirely controlled by women, continued to hate her and said later that she should have been hanged. If the abused victims during that terrible winter had complained about Renée-Pélagie, there is no evidence that she ever felt sorry for any of them. They were all working girls from working families, she was the Marquise de Sade, and there was nothing more to be said. She was even accused of deliberately placing Nanon's baby with a woman known to be pregnant, but from this the Marquise was later exonerated. The woman said her condition was due to fatigue from her work with silkworms, the local industry.

By July 1775 Madame de Montreuil was hoping that the incriminating events of the winter would be forgotten and would not damage the appeal proceedings which would presumably take place at Aix, all in due course. Everything depended on the way the young couple behaved. She did not think of her son-in-law as the only problem; her daughter was no help, she must not continue 'to compromise herself and allow him facilities unworthy of herself and of him'. However, she was not convinced of their co-operation with her: 'But are they both sensible enough to maintain this behaviour? I doubt it.' She seemed to think this was almost a case of *folie à deux*. 'And, if they are together, one will always feel justified in believing the same things and in fearing them for her whom he will drag down into the abyss with him.' Gaufridy was to do all he could to protect her from her own weakness. As usual, Madame de Montreuil ended on an emotional note: 'Her unfortunate sons who are here with me break my heart, but I can't achieve the impossible when the behaviour of the father and mother always destroys my work when it is almost completed.'

By August that year the Marquis had gone to Italy again. There was nothing else he could do. The prior of the convent who had complained about the conduct of everyone at La Coste, including the once pious Marquise, believed that her husband should be imprisoned for life. In fact the Marquis had been lucky to evade a police search at the château, and as he rode off with his valet La Jeunesse his wife was the only person in the region who believed he had been misunderstood and misjudged. She was still trying to deal with the escaped girls, who must be prevented from scandalous gossip. She herself had taken the young secretary back to his mother, who had been demanding compensation money. She had also found the money to bribe the royal prosecutor's assistant at Aix.

The Abbé at Saumane, criticized by his niece for his 'philosophical indolence', told her mother that Madame de Sade was unlikely to have any success; she was incapable of dealing with the magistrates and made a bad impression. Perhaps he was taking his revenge on the young woman who had signed blackmailing letters and involved him with the embarrassing girl who had suffered at La Coste.

Renée-Pélagie, alone again now, had to proceed with work that was far less romantic than the play-acting which had brought her, dressed in men's clothes, to the prison in Savoy. Neither was she the mere model for that arch-masochist, Justine, the pathetic heroine later created by the Marquis. She could not escape domestic detail but she was hardly the kind-hearted chatelaine who, according to her mother, had earned no complaints from the young victims of the last winter. The young people had been servants and she still treated them as such. One girl had been placed in apparent safety with Ripert (she later escaped), but the Marquise had no good sheets to send with her. Telling the steward to give her what she needed and what befitted her station, the Marquise herself sent her two chemises, two bonnets and some old shoes which she thought might be useful. Another girl who had stayed at the château developed some kind of fever, from which frequent visits from the local doctor did not help her recover. The Marquise threw her out, and two days later she died in the village. Renée-Pélagie even sacked her *valet de chambre* Jean, who had been very helpful to her for a long time. She was terrified of dangerous gossip, even from the faithful staff. Jean was to be paid off and warned not to talk or he would be sent to prison like Nanon. This was surely a new woman: she seemed at last to show some resemblance to her authoritarian mother, or even to that future Sadean heroine Juliette.

Her husband had remained irresponsible about the miserable sequel to his 'orgies'. He had spent his time reading, possibly writing and now, returning from Italy in the late summer of 1776, unpacking the works of art he had bought there – with what money is not clear – and starting to write an account of his travels. He had been quite unmoved by his wife's problems. She had been so short of money that there was no heating in the château; she caught cold because there was a broken window in her bedroom and she could not afford to have it mended. He did, however, once ask Gaufridy to send her some more fabric for clothes.

There had been a rumour that while in Italy the Marquis

had had an audience with the Pope and was now 'converted', that he had become a practising Christian. Renée-Pélagie was cynical enough to tell Gaufridy that there was no harm in the rumour. She thought it would help her husband's case when his appeal was eventually heard.

Madame de Montreuil had taken over all the necessary machinations needed for this. She was at her most magisterial herself. She was angry with everyone, telling Gaufridy early in January 1777 that she was infuriated by the treatment she received from her family – she was forced to read letters from her daughter which she knew had been dictated by Sade. 'I totally renounce taking any part in their affairs.' But if this was a serious threat at the time, it did not last. She could not resist her double battle – the domination of her own daughter and the more complex, probably sexual battle with her son-in-law. He himself acknowledged the inexplicable spell she cast over people, which always led, he was convinced, to his own victimization.

In the meantime, having completed his unpacking, the Marquis had been to explore Montpellier, seeking new 'servants', and if his wife tried to dissuade him he took no notice. He succeeded in finding a cook, a girl of twenty-two named Catherine Trillet who was the daughter of a blanket weaver. A friar had guaranteed her safety by telling her father that the château was 'a real convent'. The Marquise welcomed her, she seemed happy, and for reasons unknown her employers decided to call her 'Justine'. If Sade treated her as a sex-object she apparently had no complaints. With what money the Marquis hoped to pay a new group of servants from Montpellier, a secretary, a hairdresser, a chambermaid and a kitchen-hand, is not clear, but they too were apparently recruited by the same friar. Apparently, too, the girls were accosted by Sade during their first night at the château but refused his bribes for sexual favours. The same friar (later reprimanded by his prior) took three of them back to Montpellier at once and the news reached Catherine Trillet's father. He came to the château to demand his daughter, and the Marquise, when she heard who the visitor was, told a servant to tell her husband. There followed a confused, near-farcical incident. Catherine said she did not want to leave, Sade locked her in an adjoining room, her father took out a pistol, shot at the Marquis but missed. He then left, told the locals his version of the incident, fired another shot in the courtyard and earned the sympathy of the villagers, most of whom did not like the seigneurial ménage in any case. Later he threatened Sade with legal action and in return Sade threatened him.

Meanwhile news reached the château in January 1777 that the Dowager Comtesse de Sade in Paris was ill. The Marquis decided he must go to see her at once, and of course his wife would go with him. They left in a hurry. He took La Jeunesse and the Marquise took Catherine-Justine, who liked her employers and in any case begged Renée-Pélagie not to send her back to Montpellier. Perhaps she was afraid of her irascible father. The two women took one route to Paris, the two men another, but the reason for the segregation is not clear, unless it was thought to be safer. Somebody might have recognized the man who was in so much trouble, and if he was arrested on the way it would be better if his wife were not present.

Renée-Pélagie was never to see the Château de La Coste again. Would she be haunted later by memories of the *horreurs* that had taken place there?

5 Prisoner's Friend

I love you as one should love, excessively, madly,
with transport and despair – *Julie de Lespinasse*

℘Travelling over four hundred miles, from south to north,
in January, was of course difficult. The journey took a long
time and the four travellers, who had begun to share a carriage somewhere *en route*, did not choose a good one, for it
had constantly to be repaired and the roads were very bad.
When the two couples reached Paris on the evening of 8 February 1777, everyone was very tired. There was bad news:
'My mother-in-law died three weeks ago,' wrote Renée-Pélagie
to Gaufridy, and her husband was very upset. Before stating
these facts she had told the lawyer something more important:
they had decided not to inform her mother of the Marquis's
arrival in Paris until the following week, for on non-fasting
days la Présidente saw many people 'and would have received
bad advice'. However, she must have received intelligence reports. Renée-Pélagie, after spending one night in her late mother-
in-law's apartment at the Carmelite convent in the rue d'Enfer
(now rue Henri-Barbusse, in the 5th arrondissement), had moved
to the Hôtel de Danemark in the rue Jacob. On 13 February
Sade, who was staying with his old friend the Abbé Amblet,
came to see his wife in her bedroom. If in fourteen years of
marriage Renée-Pélagie had known her husband imprisoned

twice (plus a short period in 1771 for debt) and had visited him at Pierre-Encise, she had surely never been a witness to his arrest. But on that evening she saw Inspector Marais, who was well known in the Sade-Montreuil family, enter her room. He announced that the *lettre de cachet* he was carrying authorized him to take Sade into custody at once. There could be no argument.

The shock of the Marquis's disappearance was bad enough, but where had he been taken? Nobody would tell her, and who had told Marais that the Marquis had reached Paris? Had he fallen into a trap? Had some police spy discovered where they were both lodging and followed him when he visited her? Naturally there was a prime suspect – her mother; and just as naturally la Présidente denied everything. She persisted in saying that the arrest would help Sade: now he could be officially taken to Aix-en-Provence and his appeal against the 1772 conviction could be heard. More importantly she persisted too in saying that the arrest had nothing to do with her. Perhaps Renée-Pélagie wished she had not signed that aggressive and threatening letter to her mother which her husband had written shortly before they had both left Provence for Paris, but it was too late to regret that now. She knew she could expect no sympathy from her mother and received none. Understandably she felt that she herself should at least have been told where her husband was, for nobody would say anything, except that he was in good health. All she could do was complain to Gaufridy and repeat what she had said so often during the last few years: they must try to keep the new developments quiet in Provence. At the same time she wanted to make a protest in law about the way her husband had been arrested. Her mother, when insisting coolly that she knew nothing of the arrest, added that she was not capable of 'treason'. But Renée-Pélagie confessed – to Gaufridy, there was nobody else – that she had suffered a terrible shock and took some time to recover from it.

In the meantime it was her father, for once, not her mother, who sent the news to the Abbé de Sade at Saumane. The Abbé told Gaufridy – everyone wrote to Gaufridy – that his worries were now over and he was sure everyone would share his feelings.

Renée-Pélagie was distraught. She became convinced her husband was in the Bastille. She would have known that Voltaire had been there twice, along with other eminent people. A courtier who had threatened to publish revelations about Madame de Pompadour had been consigned to the Bastille for twenty-five years. Renée-Pélagie even went on an exploratory visit to the Bastille, but she found only drawbridges permanently raised, the guards would not even allow her to stop and look, and nobody coming out was allowed to talk. Her mother, who at least pretended not to know anything, soon found that her daughter was less 'stricken' but did not appreciate all she had done for her and her husband in trying to hasten the appeal proceedings at Aix.

In the meantime the Marquise had written to her husband, through the authorities, two days after his arrest, and continued to do so, in terms of loving devotion. She does not seem to have received a direct reply until May, and by then or soon after she had learnt where he was: at Vincennes, that gloomy fortress to the east of the city. Diderot had been there, the Comte de Mirabeau was sent there that same year by his own father, using a *lettre de cachet* in order, he maintained, to protect him against himself. Renée-Pélagie worried about her husband and would not believe he was in good shape until she could actually see him. She would look after herself well on his behalf, she wrote; he must 'do the same and count on me as your best friend whom nothing can change. Don't get into your head that people are trying to distance me from you; they know such a thing is impossible and they will not succeed'.

Madame de Montreuil wished her daughter would be more confident about her own efforts to help her son-in-law, for she believed she had been acting with moderation and sensitivity. Renée-Pélagie probably suspected that her mother was now using Gaufridy as a spy, as she had used Fage earlier, but she possibly did not know he had been instructed to pass on any news that reached him in her own letters. Madame de Montreuil regarded herself as 'a doctor working to achieve a cure', but the young couple could not accept that, and while the prisoner wrote her heartbroken or violent letters, accusing her of cruelty, she believed complacently that all was in order. Throughout this phase of Sade's detention at Vincennes Renée-Pélagie continued to write what she hoped were loving, comforting letters. While her mother wrote like a powerful lady, setting out administrative details, issuing near-aggressive instructions to everyone whom she saw as needing them, and adding a few well-placed emotional words when she believed they would be effective, her daughter wrote constantly from the heart, simple, repetitive letters, expressing all she felt for the man who was the centre of her life, her 'best friend', her lover, husband, father of her children and, in fact, a grown-up child of her own. She had often been high-handed in her letters to Gaufridy, just as she had been autocratic and uncaring in her treatment of servants like Nanon. But the often-repeated themes of her letters to her husband show a total, selfless, sometimes abject, near-masochistic devotion.

Sade was not always unresponsive. Writing on 21 April he had warned her to avoid a certain *cabinet* in her salon at the Carmelites, for ten years earlier his mother's architect had told her it could collapse. Also, he wanted to be kept up to date about her health, emphasizing that he was 'quite ready to sacrifice everything to the happiness of keeping for ever a friend like you, even the slightest health problem would reduce me to total despair'.

Renée-Pélagie could never receive enough news from him and he wrote constantly to his mother-in-law, either pleading with her or reviling her: the 'Hyena', as he and his wife called her. Renée-Pélagie had to read his miserable complaints, for there was nobody to respond to his tears and cries: 'Where is the time when my dear friend shared them? Today,' he went on, 'I no longer have anyone: it is as though all nature is dead for me!' His wife had to try to calm his fury, and he would not allow anyone to say he was mad in order to help in the presentation of his appeal. He was persistently obstinate about all aspects of the legal situation, whatever la Présidente and his wife did or tried to do. The whole situation seems to reflect a *ménage à trois*, with two apparently rival women fighting over the methods of 'helping' this difficult man. His mother-in-law worried incessantly that evidence of erotic entertainments could be found at La Coste, not only papers but 'machines', often used by libertines at the time in order to render victims helpless during sexual assault.

La Présidente even worried about a torn piece of paper that had blown away through a window at the time of the 1774 raid, but she had almost given up trying to help her daughter. She simply could not understand how she could be so blind about her husband. Surely she could see that all the accusations against him were not mere calumny? She decided not to tell her daughter too much about the background to Sade's arrest: she would allow her to be 'enlightened' by those who were not suspect. Did she have any love for her daughter? A limited love, perhaps, although she had at least said that she feared for her when she had been shut up in the Provençal château at the mercy of Sade, so she thought, and beyond the reach of any help. This organizing mother admitted to Gaufridy that her own husband had inadvertently almost given away their secret correspondence: but he saved himself just in time. Apart from her concern about the 'papers', Madame de Montreuil sounded, in all her letters, extremely complacent, and Renée-Pélagie must have envied her younger sister, Anne-Prospère, who was probably in Paris at the time, for the suffering Marquise described her mother as 'satisfied' as long as she could see her 'beautiful *dulcinée*'. As for herself, she could not wait to get out of her mother's clutches and told Gaufridy that she would rather 'plough the soil' than allow herself to fall back into them.

Renée-Pélagie wrote endless letters as the doting, over-anxious wife, worried about the prisoner's health, his food and his clothes. She ordered a grey coat from his tailor, she sent ointment for his haemorrhoids, she sent stockings, toothpicks, soap, gloves, candles, waistcoats, slippers, eau-de-Cologne and endless food – beef marrow, apricot jam, apple jelly, cherries. Whatever he asked for, she sent. Unfortunately there were two things she could not supply: the fresh air and exercise he needed so badly, and the date of his release. If she heard nothing from him she became desperate. Was he ill? 'Don't you love me any more?' Nothing could change her feelings for him, 'and the unhappiness of our present separation increases their depth'.

By early June this loving but over-optimistic wife was already writing to Gaufridy about planning a possible escape for her husband when he was eventually taken to Aix. She suggested ways of arranging it and added that no expense must be spared.

That same month she wrote about her children, how the younger boy was recovering from *la fièvre terce* (tertian fever), and how she had seen her daughter, who was at a convent school. Madeleine-Laure had indicated *politiquement* that she was pleased to see her mother but the latter assured the Marquis that the girl 'infinitely preferred the nuns to me. However, after two days we had come to know each other very well'. Renée-Pélagie was pleased on the whole but would arrange for the situation to be changed later. It looked as though mother and daughter were reliving the way Renée-Pélagie herself had probably been brought up. In September 1777 she begged her husband to change his negative moods, 'and above all love me a little. I need this consolation, and you cannot be more affected by your detention than I am as I think of all that you can be suffering, for my attachment to you has no limits'.

Letters into and out of the prison were often censored or delayed, but the Marquise busied herself with activities of the little-woman, watchful-wife type, especially when the autumn and winter made her worry about the cold in that solid stone-built edifice. Poor food was not Sade's main problem, for detainees of his class were maintained at the expense of their families. Naturally he would complain, for what else could he do? When not supplying him with clothes or luxury food, mainly sweet things, his wife was constantly writing to the minister concerned in the hope of obtaining an annulment of the Aix judgement.

Madame de Montreuil was doing the same thing. Had the

Marquis married two wives and/or acquired two mothers? In any case his mother-in-law received at least one letter written in his own blood, begging her to end his detention. It was the uncertainty which he could not tolerate. He became more and more suspicious and all his wife's attempts to instil in him the need for calm, patience and optimism were unsuccessful. The pair used invisible ink (lemon juice) in parts of their letters, until the device was discovered, Renée-Pélagie blaming herself, of course. The detainee threatened suicide, and feared he might be exiled and not allowed to see his children. She had to reassure him in November and wrote that 'whatever happens, your children and I will only leave you if you wish it'. On 3 December she answered his inquiries about the children. 'I rarely see them,' she admitted, 'I am only occupied with looking after you. I leave them entirely to the care of their grandmother. That doesn't prevent them from being worthy of your love and mine.'

As though anxious to show that the children, like the rest of the family, had not been completely taken over by la Présidente, she gave more details. Their daughter, now aged six, was still at the convent. It was too early to decide anything about her appearance or character; she was still too young. However, she may have taken after her father, for her mother referred to her 'violent' wants. 'As for your son' (that is, the elder, Louis-Marie, who was ten), he was obedient 'and remarkably lively'. He needed to be occupied, 'which is easy because he wants to know everything and would spend the whole day with books'. She thought he would become an attractive person. The younger boy, now eight, was still good-looking and docile, although he was less interested in study. He promised he would work better later, and he said this so charmingly 'that it would be cruel not to believe him. He is more loving and will be more liked in society. I always embrace him twice over because of the resemblance' – presumably to his father. 'My affection for them,' she concluded, 'brings me naturally back to you, whom I love with all my heart.'

The same day she wrote about more practical matters: Gothon, who was devotedly looking after the deserted château, had reported that the trees the Marquis had planted were growing well. The staff were to be reminded that the hazel arbour would need attention and the Marquise, although in many ways she did not regret Provence, realized how much La Coste meant to her husband. Nobody would be allowed to enter his study and Gothon was given strict orders to get rid of the rats, using any means whatever to do so. Gaufridy also kept an eye on the château and when he found a portrait affected by damp he had it rehung, with other portraits, in the gallery. Renée-Pélagie's emotional letters are still moving, some two hundred years after they were written: 'Don't thank me, my dear friend,' she wrote, 'for all that I'm sending you: this is a period that I hate. Love me well, tell me so often, that gives me pleasure and you could never say it too often.' Was ever a wife more in love? 'My consolation is to receive news of you, my consolation is to repeat endless, endless times that I love you and adore you as deeply as possible and well beyond all that can possibly be expressed.' Renée-Pélagie may have entered a marriage of convenience but she was the sort of woman who needed to give love, and to give it to one man. Perhaps too she had a desperate need to receive love in return. 'When shall I be able to embrace you? I think it will make me die of joy.' She had probably not yet read Rousseau, there is little evidence that she read anything at this period of her life, but she wrote like an unsophisticated Julie de Lespinasse, like a naïve heroine of Madame de Staël, like an unsung figure of the romantic age to come. But in a final sentence to this letter of 3 December she remembered the importance of home comforts: would he like a warm coverlet for his bed?

Although she said she did not want to be thanked, she never forgot that she wanted to be loved. Later that month she had received a list of wants from her husband but he had not added 'the slightest word of affection for me. I'm all the more sensitive about that because I'm always afraid you don't love me. This fear has always tormented me' (which explains her past behaviour to a great extent) 'but it increases now when I'm deprived of seeing you. I suffer twice over for you and for me'.

He was not to worry about her health, although she wished she could help to look after his. All that mattered was their reunion. She now described her day-to-day life in the Carmelite convent, which was not solitary. Her husband's faithful valet La Jeunesse was with her, working still as her servant, she had a chambermaid called Agathe, whom her husband knew, and a 'very fat' country girl who did the rough work. She had kept Justine for a month – Catherine-Justine whose father had tried to shoot Sade – but the girl didn't like Paris in the end and had gone back to Montpellier.

On the last day of December 1777 the Abbé de Sade died. It was Renée-Pélagie who sent out the letters informing people of the event, but the complex problems involved in the settling of the Abbé's estate belong to the biography of the Marquis.

Renée-Pélagie had asked Gaufridy to have Saumane sealed, knowing that her husband very much wanted his uncle's natural history collection and his books. (He did not get them.) She was glad to find this fatal year had ended, and in her letter of 4 January 1778 she told her husband that she was pleased at the way their children were developing. 'There's one extraordinary thing, my father loves them and you know that he does not have a very loving nature.' Which reminds us again of the atmosphere in which Renée-Pélagie had grown up. She thought the children were being taught the right things and that they would provide consolation for their father and mother. On 16 February she admitted that the children did not know where their father was; they thought he was travelling abroad. 'Your son says to me: "*Mon Dieu!* how I'd like to travel with my papa Sade!" And my reply is: "Work hard so that you'll be able to benefit from travelling with him."'

On the same day she again wrote to Gaufridy about the possible escape which must be arranged for her husband when he was taken to Aix, imagining in a fanciful way that the Aix horsemen should make their colleagues' guns and pistols damp so that they would not fire. There must be a passport prepared in advance, and letters of recommendation which would give the Marquis protection in the Republic of Venice or somewhere else. After setting out yet another cloak-and-dagger scenario she added that she was accustomed to being deceived, she was distrustful of everything.

However, she trusted in her own love for her husband, and continued to hope he loved her. She wrote to him on 17 May, the anniversary of their wedding in 1763, telling him that this was a day 'especially dear' to her. She assured him as usual that she would let him know immediately when she heard anything about his release.

No wonder she had mentioned his lack of trust, for when Sade was asked to sign the documents relevant to his appeal he wanted to hear from her that everything was in order, that he was not being led into a further trap. He even wanted her to go with him. She was told nothing; it was thought she might try to follow him to Aix, which was no doubt true. The detainee eventually signed the documents and was taken from the prison on the way to Aix on 14 June, a journey which took six days and left his wife worrying about his unexplained silence.

In the long epistolary duo which lasted from February 1777 to July 1789, Renée-Pélagie's simply written, loving letters, with all their attention to practical detail, and her husband's much more literate, self-pitying, aggressive outbursts, there were occasional changes of key, owing to outside events. The first, lasting from June to September 1778, was caused by the Marquis's journey to Aix-en-Provence and the quashing of his 1772 sentence, for which was substituted a fine, an admonition to behave better and his exclusion from Marseille for three years. Sade, as is well known, was always surrounded by women, and the faithful Gothon, hearing he was at Aix, employed her letter-writer to send him an adoring epistle, accompanied by flowers and fruit. A little later she sent him the clothes he had asked for, plus a pot of apricot jam. She wanted him back at La Coste, and no doubt she wanted La Jeunesse too, for he was her lover.

Sade's wife also wanted him back at La Coste or at least in

Paris. She had been kept in the dark as to his whereabouts because her mother was convinced she would try to join him at once – so convinced that she had contemplated placing her under guard in a convent. Renée-Pélagie was not told either that he had escaped on his way back to Paris, after the all-powerful *lettre de cachet* had frustrated his hopes for freedom. The honour of the family had been restored, but his wife's personal feelings were apparently of no importance to her mother or to anybody else. La Présidente had felt bound to take up this question of family honour because the men of the Sade family were an elderly, inactive group, and she could not resist virtually acting on their behalf. Perhaps she was all the more active because she had to avenge herself: this marriage had been her doing, and she could not tolerate the degree to which it had gone wrong.

When Renée-Pélagie eventually heard that her husband had actually escaped from his escort after his appeal, she wrote, or had sent, the joyful letter quoted in the Prologue: 'Do you believe now that I love you. . .?' Although she could do nothing for the time being to assist him, she knew how he eluded his captors at Miolans and she had hoped he would use the same skills now.

When she heard that he had actually reached La Coste, on 18 July, where he was to enjoy a month of dangerous liberty, her furious scene with la Présidente can only be imagined. Again, in her straightforward way she said her mother was 'like a lioness'. This organizing lady was not used to being defied; so far she had crushed any opposition. Ever since her daughter's reaction to the Rose Keller affair she had seen the young woman slowly gaining strength and moving away from her. She could not allow Renée-Pélagie to have ideas of her own; she had always been sure she was taking them 'parrot-fashion' from her husband. Renée realized this, and if her husband was not in the end liberated, she herself was, in a different way, although there was little she could do with the minute area of freedom she had achieved for herself. La Présidente emitted *feu et flamme*, breathed fire and smoke and kept her daughter

in Paris through financial blackmail, telling her it was dangerous for her to be shut up in La Coste with that violent man,
even though he wanted her to come, for 'a thousand reasons'.

His freedom at La Coste lasted until the small hours of 20 August,
when he was recaptured. The usually reliable Gothon had apparently failed to prepare a hiding-place for him in the roof.
On 7 September he was brought back to Vincennes. His mother-
in-law again told her daughter that she was not responsible for
his rearrest and informed Gaufridy that the Marquise should
have been allowed to see certain of those 'papers' which had
been destroyed: she would then have understood the danger of
sharing life with Sade. It is quite possible that Renée-Pélagie
knew more about these secrets than her mother realized, and in
any case, so far as is known, the violence and perversion he
had displayed were not directed against his wife. His victims
belonged invariably to the underclass of peasants or prostitutes,
and Renée-Pélagie's only involvement may have been as a spectator, an unwilling one no doubt, forming an essential part of
her support programme for the man who could do no wrong,
or no wrong she could not forgive. She insisted that she had
never been 'the director of her husband's pleasures'.

If Renée-Pélagie did not reach La Coste during her husband's
month of freedom, something, somebody from La Coste fortunately reached her, and again there was a change of key in
that continuing duo of letters.

In Paris she was isolated; she saw hardly anyone apart from
her servants and the shopkeepers who supplied her husband's
wants. Mentions of women friends in her letters are rare, and
when she heard of her husband's rearrest in the summer she
decided to write of her despair to the one woman whom she
hoped would understand. This was Marie-Dorothée de Rousset,
a spinster of thirty-four who had known Sade when they were
children. She was the daughter of a notary from Apt and had
met the Marquise on visits to La Coste when the family were
in residence. During Sade's month of liberty in the summer
she had been at the château, an unhappy spectator of his rearrest.
Renée-Pélagie, now at her wit's end, and receiving letters from

her husband full of invective and hatred, saying he never wanted to see her and her horrible children again, and so on, wrote in despair to Marie-Dorothée: 'Whom can I trust? What can I believe?' She said she no longer saw her mother and 'I've sworn to her in writing eternal hatred and vengeance if, within three days, she does not arrange for me to rejoin my husband wherever she has had him transferred.' Her mother had asked a third party to reply, claiming that she didn't know what her daughter meant. Nobody would tell the Marquise anything, she desperately needed advice and hoped Marie-Dorothée would come to stay with her soon.

Sade continued to write the most 'sadistic' letters he ever composed, and in her replies his wife usually chose to ignore the worst of them, assuming they represented his total frustration and his attempt to 'escape'. Fortunately she did not see at the time the cruel and sometimes obscene notes he added to her letters when he received them. She kept all this correspondence carefully and in May 1779 she wrote cheerfully what she would do when he was released: she would lock him in her bedroom and make him read all the letters he had written to her from prison. He would be forced to admit his errors. It was one of her gentle, indirect ways of complaining about his behaviour.

She dealt with many business matters and his endless demands and complaints as though quite unmoved, adding her usual protestations of love: 'You may count on me,' she wrote on 28 September, 'as on a second self, loving you as ever with a tenderness far above all expression.' She needed a woman at her side, a woman who was virtually of her own class, not an aristocrat, and who better than someone who had known the Marquis most of her life, someone who was not distracted by emotional problems of her own? Despite her endless difficulties Renée-Pélagie was still ready to mother her guest; she asked her husband to let her know if Mademoiselle de Rousset had a favourite meal and whether she preferred dinner or supper. She herself was on a diet but did not want to inflict it on her guest. While waiting for her to arrive, Renée-Pélagie told her husband that their sons were to spend two years at Vallery, near Sens, at a country house owned by their grandparents, who adored them. A local prior, the curé of Vallery, *un homme d'esprit*, would act as tutor to them. A mention of their father was struck out by the prison censor but 'the elder boy ... often looked at your portrait, which pleased me very much. The chevalier [the younger boy] also looked at it a good deal, but he didn't recognize you so easily; he was so little when you left us! They told me that they very much wanted to see you and to live with us'. Their mother remained hopeful, as ever: 'I told them that when they came back I promised them they would join you and me again, in whatever country we were.' And did her husband want the faithful governess, Madame Langevin, to take over their daughter now, so that she would not spend her life in the convent?

Mademoiselle de Rousset finally arrived on 6 November and stayed with the Marquise at the Carmelite convent. She found her hostess very thin, for she had been ill earlier, but nothing could stop Renée-Pélagie from being over-kind and attentive to her guest, who wanted to do something for her in return. She wanted also to 'shake her up a little.' Marie-Dorothée's presence had two effects on the separated ménage: the fascinating correspondence, amusing, quasi-erotic and finally bad tempered, between herself and the detainee belongs to the latter's biography and has often been quoted, but it is her relationship with Renée-Pélagie that concerns us here, as well as the difficult relationship between the Marquise and her mother. Since Renée-Pélagie was uniquely occupied with obtaining her husband's release, Marie-Dorothée naturally tried to help in this insoluble situation. She even went to see Madame de Montreuil, whom she called 'the high priestess', and both women left accounts of the interview. It would be hard to find two more different people: the Provençal spinster, surprisingly well educated, eccentric, dedicated to both Sade partners, and the Parisian *maîtresse femme*, intent on organizing her family, including even her relations by marriage, while her ambiguous relationship with her son-in-law had estranged her from her eldest daughter, whom she affected to love but probably didn't.

Marie-Dorothée left the best description ever written of this clever and powerful lady: she was 'a charming woman... still very youthful, short rather than tall, with a pleasant face, a seductive laugh and expression, an impish mind, the wisdom and frankness of an angel, as subtle as a fox, however, but amiable and seductive in her way'. She had one thing in common with the Marquis: she had made her conquest, Marie-Dorothée reported to Gaufridy. Clearly la Présidente defended her own position *vis-à-vis* the Marquis with brilliance, but at least the younger woman said, 'modestly', that yes, she would speak up for Sade, even though she was reminded of his many broken promises. Without going to the lengths of Renée-Pélagie in his defence, she said: 'Men are weak, Madame, you know; age and his misfortunes have produced great changes....'

She tried to tell the Marquis in her letters that nothing could be hurried, that his wife was mistaken in thinking that it could, but unfortunately she could not change the attitude of either partner. She often wrote to the prisoner in the firm, humorous way that she hoped Renée-Pélagie might adopt, but the latter was not ready for change. If her husband knew how much pleasure they found in packing the basket they sent to the prison every fortnight, he would not be so critical of its contents, she said. She would never have dared say to him, as her friend did, 'How crazy women are to attach themselves to an awkward customer like you!' They rushed to carry out all his wishes, they tried to do everything for the best, but 'Monsieur was never satisfied.' Marie-Dorothée realized that he always had to be handled with care, it was dangerous to rub him up the wrong way – something his uncle the Abbé had realized years earlier. Marie-Dorothée always wrote in a forthright, semi-sarcastic style that could hardly be more different from that of her hostess. 'Don't scold him,' the Marquise told her. 'I beg you, he's unhappy.' But then she described how her friend could help this miserable man – she must tell him funny stories and make him laugh. That was something Renée-Pélagie could not do, she was too frightened that he would purposely misunderstand anything she wrote and try to find in her words some of those 'signals' he looked for so desperately, hidden clues that spelt out the date of his release. Marie-Dorothée – Sainte Rousset, as Sade and his wife called her – said what she wanted to say and teased him, giving her opinion of men in general as a poor set of creatures and telling him: 'Along with our lovers and the pleasure of good company we do you the honour of thinking about you sometimes.' His wife, she told him, was well, apart from being thin. Occasionally she suffered from haemorrhoids, but he was not to worry about that. 'She eats, she sleeps, she loves you.' In an attempt to occupy this wife whose empty existence was becoming so negative, Marie-Dorothée had suggested she should learn to play the guitar, and persuaded a friend of her own to teach her. A few lessons would kill time. She had forgotten that the idea of another man in the house would make Sade jealous, but she hastened to reassure him: the teacher was a very respectable man, they did not see him very often, for he was too busy, but she liked to hear Madame playing: 'at least I know she isn't bored'.

In fact both Renée-Pélagie and Sade himself were stimulated by Marie-Dorothée's visit. Books were discussed: the 'Sainte' explained to the prisoner why she had been unable to read Samuel Richardson's *Clarissa Harlowe*, she criticized a poem he had written in Provençal, and the two women read together the letters they sent and received. The Marquise affected at least to be jealous when her friend amused herself by making declarations of love to her husband, in Provençal.

But she was more than grateful for the presence of her guest – 'she makes me laugh, she makes me eat'. Marie-Dorothée's taste for plain speaking eventually made it easier for her friend to be honest about family matters. For instance, Marie-Dorothée took a great interest in little Madeleine-Laure, who was now seven, and saw the child on days when she was allowed out of the convent. When she described her to her father, his suspicions were realized: she was plain. Renée-Pélagie now began to be more honest about her, and there was worse news still:

'. . . my good friend,' she wrote on 10 December 1778, 'as for your daughter, you've guessed right, she squints. But since a mother is always blind about her daughter, don't go by what I tell you'. She thought, well in advance, that she had better become a secular canoness, for she would have no dowry. (Did she remember her own sister, of whom there was temporarily no news?) Writing later she thought she would be less ugly as she grew up, and would not belie her name – Sade was always conscious of his distant ancestor by marriage, Petrarch's Laura, who had married Hugues de Sade three centuries earlier. Her mother had decided to tolerate the nuns, who did not allow many outings, for otherwise the convent seemed good.

Marie-Dorothée seemed to understand and like the little girl, who resembled her father in looks, she thought, but unlike him she soon proved to be a slow learner. Marie-Dorothée helped her compose a letter to her father, and her mother was shocked to discover that she could hardly write at all. She blamed her teacher, but said, characteristically, that she would have to be patient, and as soon as her husband was released she would take action to improve the situation. The child wasn't wasting her time, her knowledge of religion was good, the social graces could be learnt quickly. She also described why she had better stay at the convent for the time being: she needed 'to learn how to live with others, for she has the defect of wanting everything to give way to her wishes and to be in no way understanding of others'. She did not take after her mother. At the end of April 1779 this mother described how she was dressed. She was trying to tell her husband everything about his youngest child, of whom he had seen very little. The poor girl wore a sheath-like garment, 'a kind of English dress, puce, near-violet in colour, a jabot and the rest in linen or muslin'. She also wore a bonnet. Renée-Pélagie's own education had probably not been very different.

How much she herself read is not clear, but she did mention that she had read the Abbé de Sade's work on Petrarch, and during the spring of 1779 she became preoccupied with her husband's requests for books, some of them classics like

Plutarch, about which she had to take advice from the Abbé Amblet. She also had to find the later volumes of a work very popular at the time, *Le voyageur français* by the Abbé Joseph de la Porte, who had begun to publish it in 1765. The prisoner was also anxious to have a new edition of the complete works of Voltaire, sixty volumes in all, but the subscription was very expensive.

Sade never stopped complaining about the food and clothing his wife sent him, but at least he seemed to be spending more time in reading or writing, especially since the liberal-minded minister Malesherbes had decreed that prison governors could now be more tolerant in these matters. Sade asked continually for weighty tomes, especially histories of all types, their subjects including the Inquisition, Mexico and the Celts, three volumes of a work on famous women, many plays, Fontenelle's important work *Entretiens sur la pluralité des mondes habités*, to name but a few.

The preoccupation with books reduced Renée-Pélagie's anguish a little. The detainee had even suggested she wrote less because her letters were so boring. She replied that she could not bear to write less. She told him to read with his heart and not with his head.

If Renée-Pélagie was no great reader and much less educated than her husband and friend, many books now passed through her hands as she struggled round bookshops and libraries trying to find the wanted titles, asking for help from the faithful Abbé Amblet. She knew that everything she sent would be seen first by the prison censors, and she tried to anticipate their reaction. Rousseau's *Confessions*, for instance, would be banned. Rousseau was far from popular with the authorities and after *Émile* (which had been burnt) he had had to flee to Switzerland. Most of the *Confessions* was not published officially until after his death in 1788, copies being circulated privately. Renée-Pélagie began to understand libraries and other lenders who would harass her to send books back, and she found that the most recently performed plays were not yet printed.

Her own life was enriched in one way when Sade, the one-time amateur actor and producer, now began to pass the time by writing plays himself, copied usually by La Jeunesse, who had a good hand and could spell, sometimes by Renée-Pélagie herself, although her handwriting was not very readable and her spelling infantile and phonetic. She at least read the plays and surprisingly perhaps she did not react like so many writers' wives by finding everything perfect, although she admitted she was partial. For instance on 16 December 1780 she reported on his five-act prose play *Henriette de Saint-Claire*: 'I find it basically good and written in a way to make the greatest impression on those who have a soul. It will revolt cowardly souls who will not understand the position and the situation.' The theme of the play was one which preoccupied Sade in many of his writings: incest. She added that it was sufficiently different from Diderot's *Le père de famille* not to seem like a copy. In March 1781 she was about to read the second version of her husband's play *Les deux jumelles*: 'The first version seemed to me very honest and could be acted in a convent, it's rather cold, but it's not bad; it seemed cold to me only because your style, in your work as in other things, scorches the paper.' The wife who had spent all her time dispatching luxury food, clothes and the very necessary candles and paper to the prison was practical enough to become a sound and commonsensical reader for her husband. It must have been many years since she had been in a theatre – probably not since her honeymoon – but surely she had not forgotten the amateur theatricals in which she had taken part, which was just as well, for her husband perpetually dramatized his own situation and for what seemed like an eternity the separated couple were condemned to a life of dialogue made more dramatic still by the intervention of the prison censor.

Later Marie-Dorothée was to make some discoveries about the prisoner and his 'crimes' which were theatrical too, in a different way. Meanwhile, in that spring of 1781, Renée-Pélagie thought she had achieved something that her husband would appreciate and even thank her for. With the help of Madame de Sorans, a lady-in-waiting to the King's sister, Madame Elisabeth, she had arranged for the detainee to be transferred to the prison fortress of Crest, which stood between Valence and Montélimar in the Rhône valley, for he had so often pleaded to be closer to his estates at La Coste. He had even hoped for temporary release in order to supervise them. But nobody could help the man who was his own worst enemy: he seems to have thought about the transfer but in the end he refused to go, saying the place stood in the middle of a swamp and was infested with rats. His wife, as usual, did not show too much disappointment, but her letter of 5 April proves that she had at least learnt how to tell him what she thought: he was delaying the pleasure of their meeting. 'I repeat, your schemes and calculations have always been false, utterly false and more than absurd. For once in your life have confidence in those whom you should trust and get ready to go. I've nothing more to say to you.'

But she was pleased about one thing: even if Sade had turned down the Montélimar proposal she had made her mother very angry, for the idea had been her own. Madame de Montreuil could not tolerate any show of initiative on the part of her daughter. A month later Renée-Pélagie was writing to acknowledge the receipt of a new play in manuscript, *Le capricieux* – and would he send some money, for she had none.

In order to save expense she had moved out of the Carmelite convent to the rue de la Marche in the Marais, and Marie-Dorothée stayed in another convent close by. Her friend was about to leave for Provence. She had already postponed the journey for two reasons: she did not want to desert the Marquise and she was perhaps still hopeful of seeing her old friend, even in prison, but her own health had deteriorated. She had begun to spit blood, and it was La Jeunesse, the valet, not Renée-Pélagie, who prepared 'horrible' beverages for her, no doubt herbal concoctions of some sort. Mademoiselle de Rousset had done all she could for Renée-Pélagie, she had even braved the 'Hyena' once again – the 'heroine of deception', as she described her to Gaufridy. She had written to her about business difficulties (Sade refused to authorize his wife to act on his behalf in various legal matters), 'the danger of a long detention and finally the deterioration in her daughter's health'. La Présidente replied briefly with a somewhat angry letter, saying that she thought 'I would have calmed her daughter's mind and heart.' Marie-Dorothée had lost much of her early feeling for the 'Hyena' and told Gaufridy what she had obviously been told by Renée-Pélagie's helpmate Agathe. 'Her hatred is concealed with great art. . . . When her daughter was ill, but seriously ill (it was before I arrived), she came to see her, remained with her for a moment, went from the cellar to the attic, saw the *femme de chambre*, who has been with her ever since her marriage to Monsieur de Sade, and said to her, haughtily: "It is unfortunate for my daughter that her heart is so taken up with her husband." Agathe replied: "My goodness! It's quite natural that she loves a husband who has always treated her well." This answer incurred the indignation of the dowager lady, she criticized everything: "That has not been swept; that box has not been put away; that saucepan is not clean, good day, take care of my daughter."'

Marie-Dorothée thought these details would help Gaufridy to see what la Présidente was like, especially since he was now known to be working for her. She added details which illuminate further the wretchedness of Renée-Pélagie's situation, for her mother had apparently persuaded all the members of the Montreuil family to agree with her about a long detention for Sade. 'One of Madame's maternal uncles wrote to her for New Year's Day: "You are wrong to be angry with your family," he said, "it is you who should be blamed for accepting so much from your husband. You should remember that you have brothers and sisters who must be settled, etc." If all that crowd has to be married before he can be freed, I assure you that this would be excessive.' It was an uncle who had written this reproving letter, not an aunt, for only a man's attitude would be taken seriously, and for 'settled' (*établi*) one had to read 'married', and that applied to both daughters and sons.

The prisoner's wife already had enough to contend with.

Nobody except Marie-Dorothée was on her side, but her love for her husband never faltered, while it remained inextricable from her feelings for her mother. Once, when Renée-Pélagie was experiencing some hope, there had been talk of a box made from lava which the Marquis would give personally to his mother-in-law when he was free, but such optimism never lasted long. On one occasion la Présidente called on her daughter without being announced by any servant, and the Marquise, taken by surprise, was even affectionately polite to her. While the younger woman was collecting some papers – accounts, naturally – from another room, la Présidente took the opportunity to talk to Marie-Dorothée and attack her son-in-law, explaining how much she had done for him and how much of his capital he had spent. Her daughter's friend tried to support both partners.

'"Madame," I said to her, "you must forget the past and be concerned only with the means of ensuring everything for the future; they are your children, they should be dear to you, you know in spite of yourself that you're their mother."'

'"I love my daughter," she said, "I have a mother's gut feeling for her, there is no more to be said."'

Marie-Dorothée apparently showed her indignation in silence. She told her friend later that she was perhaps pleading a very bad cause but *amour-propre* led her to cling to her firm opinion to the end.

October 1780 had brought serious revelations that the cause was indeed bad, worse than she had expected. Following pleas by Renée-Pélagie and manoeuvres by her mother, various people in power, including the minister Maurepas and his wife, were examining Sade's case in detail. Even two princesses had apparently intervened on his behalf. Marie-Dorothée had persuaded some official to take a risk and show a friend and herself the relevant papers which revealed the true reasons for his detention. Reading them gave her a fever for several days, for it was now apparent to her that 'the dear présidente was not as guilty as we had thought'. Marie-Dorothée thought she owed it to the Marquise to speak frankly, but she was hardly successful. Both Sade partners were impossible – if only Renée-Pélagie had 'more education, more greatness of soul ... those natural and sensitive feelings acquired at birth and maintained by virtue and justice until death'. Why did she not stand up to that man? Sade himself, whom she had now 'examined and dissected', had such a 'baroque nature' that he inspired more pity than anger and sadly enough his wife was partly responsible: 'I'm no longer astonished that the unfortunate man has done so many stupid things; he needed someone with muscle; this person has only fibres or filaments spun and woven by spiders.' Marie-Dorothée had seen how her friend could not even be strict with her maid Agathe and, more importantly, Renée-Pélagie continued, against all odds, to believe in her husband and forgive him everything. Was it a case of *folie à deux*, even in separation, was she the only kind of wife he could have tolerated, could her situation be summed up in the title of Dryden's play: *All for Love or the World Well Lost*?

Marie-Dorothée could not refrain from telling Gaufridy in her usual dramatic way what she had learnt after the would-be supporters had studied all the papers relevant to Sade's continued detention. 'He is all right where he is,' they had apparently said, 'his wife is mad or as guilty as he is to dare ask for his freedom. We do not want to see her.' Not only was the Marquise condemned to social ostracism, but even her good friend from Provence had been influenced by what she had learnt. 'The man should be hanged!' she wrote on 23 October to Gaufridy. Three weeks later she returned to the theme: Madame de Sade was still hopeful: '... such is her folly! She has seen and heard'. She had not listened to her friend's wise counsel. Every day she would say: 'When Monsieur is out we'll do, we'll say, etc.' Marie-Dorothée would either laugh or shrug her shoulders. Sometimes she would sing, her hostess would doze off, they would attend to their clothes, eat and sleep. It was a dull life, contrasting strongly with the Parisian gaiety that continued all around them. Marie-Dorothée wanted to go back to Provence; she could not stand this situation any longer. She talked vaguely of leaving the following spring, but her hostess did not want to believe her. The visitor knew too that the Montreuil family regarded her as a *bête noire*, for she at least seemed to support their daughter's crazy ideas.

In the meantime there were no developments in the Sade ménage except the detainee's growing interest in reading and writing. He did not stop his letter-writing but interrupted it occasionally in order to cause anxiety about his health or state of mind; he inflicted emotional cruelty on his wife just as in the past he had whipped the street-girls he chose for the purpose. Just occasionally he would allow her a moment's appreciation: he would write a few quasi-erotic lines about 'measuring' themselves and each other; he would tell Marie-Dorothée, but not Renée-Pélagie, that he knew such wives were not made any more, 'and I beg you to preserve her for me'.

In April 1780 Renée-Pélagie had seemed to show something more of the confidence that had been slowly growing in her mind: 'You embrace me more tenderly than I do, *bien sûr*, you say! To tell you the truth, without hurting your feelings, I doubt it rather, my dear friend.' He seemed to be hoping for a warmer response: 'Don't worry about my laconic style,' she wrote in June 1780. 'I still adore you and neglect nothing which could be of value to you. Be calm, don't worry about anything and don't get any wild idea into your head. I embrace you.' While sending him more books, plus eel pâté, game of all kinds, from pheasants to thrushes, and marshmallow syrup, she told him that when he was released he could go round the bookshops himself and see that it was not her fault if the wanted books could not always be found.

She was touched when he remembered her fête-day and grateful when he inquired about the children. She had told Madeleine-Laure that her father was travelling in Spain but could no longer think what to tell the two boys, for he had not written to them for a long time. He did take an interest, however, and she told him all the details. The elder boy had made good progress in Latin, knew his mythology and the related history, he was beginning Greek, he read a lot, his writing was so like his father's that it could be mistaken for it. He was as tall as his mother, he talked too fast and he wanted to go into the army and wear a uniform. He was thirteen. The two brothers were fond of each other. The younger boy, now eleven, was better looking and everyone embraced him. Although he was intelligent he was very lazy about school work. Both boys had had smallpox but had not suffered greatly and the younger boy had only red marks on his skin as a result. Their sister, she wrote later, had had smallpox twice when she was very young but she was now very well, apart from her bad teeth. Their mother always enthused about her children but she had to make sacrifices: she would not go to see them in the country while their father was in Vincennes and needing her close to him, but fortunately she had been able to spend a week with them because they had been brought close to Paris to study with a tutor who kept a *pension*. She justified her entire behaviour through her belief in her husband: if, through any means whatever, she could hasten his release, then her children would benefit. Again she defended her 'laconic' style, and for a very good reason: '... when I wrote to you in more detail you always saw things in my letters which I had no intention of putting there'. She didn't want him to get upset and his 'happiness and peace of mind' were dearer to her than her life. She had been surprised to hear that he was writing a book about metempsychosis, for she thought nothing of the concept. However, all the ideas he told her about, all the books he asked her to find, were the foundation for his writing. Perhaps he discussed his plans with the Abbé Amblet, and sometimes he asked his old tutor for precise opinions on his plays, but he had only one reliable researcher, one reader, especially after Mademoiselle Rousset's departure – his wife. Who else was there to help him, apart from La Jeunesse, who copied his manuscripts? Renée-Pélagie wanted to save her husband. She perhaps did not know that she was helping to create a writer. She did know that this husband was a man apart, and in one lyrical moment she had told him in a letter that he was perfect in most things, if only he would not be suspicious, hot-headed, extreme in everything and sometimes given to writing things that were *peu convenables*, not respectable. But she added that he would always be perfect for her.

In early summer she had to carry out an embarrassing commission for him, for reading, writing and eating had not been adequate substitutes for his sexual drive. Fetishism had not been enough either. She had sent at his request the sleeve from a dress she had worn, but he was now reduced to constant masturbation and asked her to obtain for him a 'flask', for obvious purposes. She failed to understand why he wanted it to be so big; he couldn't put it in his pocket. He wrote a note on the back of her letter – it was not for putting in his pocket. He kept on giving her precise instructions and she kept on going back to the suppliers. Perhaps she did grasp in the end what this was all about, for in a letter of 11 July 1781 she mentioned *prestiges* and *chimères*, which in Sadian language had sexual connotations. Significantly she then went on to say she was convinced their happiness would return. She urged him to rise above all their problems: 'Let us show that we are greater than our persecutors and brace ourselves against adversity.' She said that he must agree to the reasonable propositions she would tell him when they met, for a couple of words were more worthwhile than years of writing. Her attempts to obtain the mysterious 'flasks' and their cases went on for years; the craftsmen making them would laugh at her. But she told her husband that when she saw him she would tell him a funny story about them.

If her attempt to arrange Sade's transfer to Montélimar had failed because of his obstinacy, her tireless efforts to obtain more exercise for him had been successful, and in July 1781 she was at last allowed to see him.

6 Prison Visitor

Life resembles novels more than novels resemble
life. – *George Sand*

Renée-Pélagie's last sight of her husband had been over
four years earlier, in January 1777 when he had been arrested in her hotel bedroom in the rue Jacob. On that occasion the Marquis was not yet thirty-seven years old, still agile
enough to escape from his guards at Valence the following
year. Now in the *salle de conseil* at Vincennes, with a prison
officer in the background, she found a balding man of forty-
one who had grown unattractively fat, because he had spent
the last few years eating rich and mainly sweet foods and had
not had enough exercise. She had worked hard to obtain this
and other privileges for him, but his behaviour had been too
bad, he lost any favours as quickly as he earned them.

For almost four years this wife had been writing to her husband
telling him how much she loved him and longed to see him
again. On that July day she did what surely any wife, any woman
would have done, she tried to look her best, although she was
never vain or fashionable. Where would she have found the
money for new clothes? It was the prisoner who ordered new
outfits, everything from coats to stockings and boots, all packed
and delivered under her supervision, and paid for with difficulty.

Characteristically she expected too much from this irascible, obsessed, frustrated man. Her friend Marie-Dorothée had warned her against any optimism. Their meeting would not solve all problems, she had said. In fact it created more. In mid-August he wrote her a shattering letter, a follow-up apparently of an earlier one. He complained bitterly about her appearance, the most obvious form of cruelty he could think of at the time: he accused her of looking like a 'mountebank or a seller of quack medicines'. Would she have gone to Easter communion dressed like that? he asked, presumably equating himself with the deity or at least with a festive church occasion. He didn't care how other women dressed – following others had been her earlier excuse, for this was the period of ultra-sophisticated fashion in Paris and elsewhere – he wanted her to dress like a woman of sixty. Their misfortunes, he claimed, were taking them close to that age. Evidently he wanted no sign of femininity, no hint of sexual appeal. He wanted to see her in a dark, high-necked dress, not one that was white and low-cut. He wanted no false curls, no chignon or long tresses, and she must wear a very large bonnet. If she looked like an attractive woman, presumably men would notice her, and he would not allow that. He wrote several pages, moving from fury to jealousy and pathos. He even suspected her of infidelity with the police officer Boucher, who had probably been present at the interview. He could not tolerate an unfaithful wife, he said, his jealousy was 'a slow poison' to him; his only consolation had been the happy old age they would spend together. At the end of that famous 'long letter' he had written in February 1781, a not very convincing apologia for all his so-called 'crimes', he had said that he would love her until he died. Now, he said, moving from *vous* to *tu,* he would rather die in prison than come out to see 'infamy, yours and that of the monsters who advise you'. It was a typical irrational outburst, but surely Renée-Pélagie would never dare to wear a white dress at Vincennes again, for her husband said that if she did, he would refuse to see her. He ended on a warmer note. He needed to see her alone; he begged her to arrange it.

She perhaps did not realize how the prisoner would be affected by a glimpse of the outside world, the world denied to him.

She too had been affected by the meeting, shocked now by the accusation of infidelity, for surely no woman in the whole of Paris was less inclined to respond to *galanterie* at any level. She assured him that Boucher would not reappear and at least she was capable of seeing the funny side of all this: 'I can't prevent myself from laughing as I write at the wildness of your suspicions, but I am truly upset that you suspect me of such things and that you torture yourself over such crazy fancies.'

But her husband must have wanted to be jealous. It was one of his ways, perhaps, of telling her that he loved her. He now accused her of taking a lover, one Lefèvre from Provence who had earlier been taught to read and write by the Abbé de Sade, later becoming secretary to the Marquis in 1771 and 1772. After working in Aix-en-Provence he had come to Paris to better himself and there he helped Renée-Pélagie. His portrait, by Marie-Dorothée, had reached Vincennes, and Sade in a jealous fury now slashed it thirteen times with a knife, added drops of blood and framed it with obscene annotations. He even calculated the length of Lefèvre's penis. He accused Renée-Pélagie of being pregnant by this harmless man and made a point of stressing his peasant origins.

The long-suffering Marquise, whom her husband had already compared to a notorious prostitute of the preceding century, told Marie-Dorothée about this incident, expressing her despair, but eventually the crisis passed. (Much later, in the early nineteenth century, Lefèvre became Sub-Prefect of Verdun and published a study on eloquence, but the Sade ménage never showed any interest in how a peasant, helped by some basic education, could so easily rise in the fast-changing eighteenth-century world. A little paternalism was in order, but nothing more, and a servant must remain a servant.) Strangely, the portrait of Lefèvre is one of the very few authentic images that have survived from the entourage of the Sade family.

This was not the last time the prisoner was jealous. One of Renée-Pélagie's few friends, the Marquise de Villette, who had recently lost her daughter, offered her lodging, and Renée-Pélagie, tempted by this sign of friendship, told her husband about it.

The Villette ménage was an unusual one: the Marquis, a cousin of Madame de Sade, had married a woman twenty years younger than himself who had been befriended by Voltaire and his niece. The marriage did not cure him for long of his homosexual preferences and Sade, knowing this, told his wife that the Marquise herself was promiscuous and *'un peu* Sapho' [*sic*]. In fact Renée-Pélagie was instructed to have nothing more to do with her lonely and well-meaning friend, despite the help given by the Marquis de Villette in finding books for Sade. So the prisoner destroyed one of the few friendships his wife could enjoy and she, typically, told him that in any case she made friends only in order to help him.

The year 1781 was not as good as it might have been, for prison visits and even letters were stopped when the detainee behaved badly. The prison governor found Sade so violent that he even thought him capable of attacking his wife in a fury. She was asked to explain the reasons for his jealousy, which she found humiliating, but she must have secretly pleased Sade when she descended into the depths of masochism: 'If I were allowed to see you and you were capable of thrusting a dagger into me, it would be a great happiness for me in these circumstances to exist no longer.' She could have been Justine, the long-suffering heroine who must have already taken shape in Sade's mind. At the time he wrote a heartless note on the back of her letter: *Quelle platitude, grand Dieu! Quelle platitude!*

There had been other bad news that year, evidence of which is contained in a letter to Gaufridy, who was still the centre for interfamily communication. On 24 May Marie-Dorothée had written to the lawyer: the Marquise wished to inform him of the illness and sudden death on 13 May of Mademoiselle de Launay, her sister. The death was thought to have been caused by a combination of smallpox and what today would be called peritonitis. 'Pray for her,' wrote Mademoiselle de Rousset. 'Madame de Montreuil is said to be inconsolable. Madame is afraid she will make herself ill. Tomorrow she will enter this house of grief to mingle her tears with those of the family.' The eldest daughter remained dutiful therefore, but there is no indication that she was reconciled with her mother. Neither did she tell her husband of the death, refusing to remind him of those early emotional adventures which had involved all three of them. Back in 1779 she had told him her sister was not married, 'and I shall not go to her wedding'. It was 1787 before she gave some mysterious answers to questions about Anne-Prospère that he had put to her:

For what reason did she leave my mother's house?

None that concerns you or dishonours her.

Is she my enemy?

No.

How is she living, without naming the street or the district?

Whatever it is, that cannot cause you any harm.

When Sade died, a miniature portrait of Anne-Prospère was found in his room at Charenton. There was no portrait of her elder sister. When Anne-Prospère had corresponded in Provence with the Abbé de Sade, she had written: 'You are very fortunate, my uncle, to be in your solitude, given over to yourself; as for me, I should like only that; Paris bores me, society exhausts me. . . .' She wanted only to be in her apartment 'where I withdraw as often as possible and study alone distracts me from the sufferings of my life'.

Her sufferings were over early. Those of her sister continued, for she decided she must get herself to a nunnery, for the sake of economy but more seriously to silence her husband's jealous suspicions, 'in order to stop you from tormenting yourself as you do'. She eventually chose the Augustine convent of Sainte-Aure, in the rue Neuve-Sainte-Geneviève, now the rue Tournefort in the 5th arrondissement, where Marie-Dorothée had stayed earlier. One previous resident had become well known, if hardly popular: Jeanne Bécu, later Madame du Barry, after living there from the age of ten to fifteen, was sent away for being rude and lazy. However, the Marquise told the prisoner on 10 September that she was happy there, although the regime was strict and the food was meagre, just sufficient to keep her alive. Some women would not be pleased with it, but she did not mind and did not take the religious practices too seriously.

She did not see much of the nuns and her apartment, on the first floor, was the best in the house – next to the bakery, apparently.

If her husband was in a prison cell Renée-Pélagie, despite her three convent rooms, could almost have been in prison herself. She hardly went out, except to visit bookshops, libraries, purveyors of fine foods (nothing but the best for the detainee), and Sade's tailor, Carlier, in the rue Saint Nicaise. She received an occasional visitor, but there was no one who could accompany her to the theatre or other entertainments. Sometimes she was lucky enough to see her children, but since her mother was usually involved in any such meeting her pleasure was limited. She no doubt read the gazettes or *Le Mercure de France*, from which La Jeunesse cut out and kept articles likely to interest the Marquis on his release, but she rarely mentioned outside events in her letters. That would not have pleased the prison censors and Sade would surely have misinterpreted anything he read. She had seen a few extra people during Marie-Dorothée's stay with her, but after her departure they also faded from her life. 'My taste is truly for solitude,' she wrote, as though echoing those early words of her sister. She tried every method she could think of to subdue her husband's jealousy and bitter obsessions. She tried to look more deeply into his mind, upset at the way he tried to persuade himself that she was always in the wrong. 'Through imagining it, you will believe it, and that makes me despair.' She wanted him to look into his heart in good faith. He had to believe her. She knew she was innocent and had done nothing that was not intended to help him, but that was not enough for her; she could not be calm until he admitted in good faith that she was in the right.

The autumn of 1781 brought news of another death, this time from La Coste. Gothon, realizing that her lover La Jeunesse was not going to return to her, had married Jacques Grégoire, a local carpenter much younger than herself, and had even given up her lifelong Protestantism to do so. A week after their baby was born Gothon died of puerperal fever, despite the devoted nursing of Marie-Dorothée de Rousset. Renée-Pélagie gave few obvious signs of regret, and she had earlier decided that Gothon had not been the faithful and honest housekeeper she had once thought. She was more concerned with scolding Marie-Dorothée for risking her own health and with the practical steps that should now be taken: all Gothon's possessions must be burnt, sold or set apart; the château must be fumigated by burning juniper.

At that period anyone who was converted to Catholicism received a pension from the State and Renée-Pélagie, no doubt seeking reimbursement for Gothon's neglect of the château, asked for it to be paid to her. It was left to the Marquis to write a kind of epitaph for the girl who had granted him sexual favours, sent him flowers and affectionate letters. He wanted any debts paid and Gaufridy was to give Marie-Dorothée some money so that there could be a little service in the parish for her. He knew she had her faults, but she was *'une bonne fille'*. *'Je la regrette,'* he wrote. He added that if she had taken anything out of the château, it should be returned.

Mademoiselle de Rousset was persuaded to keep an eye on La Coste for the absent owners, and her description of it in 1781 does not say much for Gothon's housekeeping. The state of the kitchens was particularly lamentable, the saucepans were covered with verdigris, they would 'make thirty-six cats vomit', the frying-pans and coffee-pots were full of holes, there were no knives, it would be dangerous even to cook an egg. When the Marquise had lived at the château she would rarely have seen the kitchens, which were the domain of the servants. She herself was not expected to be domesticated, even if she was practical. Of all the tools there remained only one wretched hammer – the garden tools had all gone. Marie-Dorothée, whose own health was rapidly deteriorating, had bravely gone to live in the château, but she found worms in the feather beds, tiles fell regularly from the roof and trees were being cut down by intruders. Renée-Pélagie urged replanting, but who would supervise the work, who would pay for it? The Marquis isolated in Vincennes, the Marquise isolated in the convent, the château in a state of decay: the situation seemed to symbolize the collapse of the *ancien régime*.

In the meantime, in Paris, the dialogue of the almost deaf continued. Renée-Pélagie was hoping to have her portrait painted by Van Loo, who was very successful and popular at the time, but one thing prevented her. It would cost ten louis and she was still short of money. She added, characteristically, that her husband would have the children's portraits, and eventually they were all completed by someone no doubt much cheaper than Van Loo, a woman, who was described as *la peintresse*.

In the meantime the children, at least the boys, had begun to grow up. Renée-Pélagie assured their father that they loved him. They must surely have absorbed her affection for him before they were born, she said. Louis-Marie was fourteen and on his way to the army. He and his younger brother, who later joined the religious military organization of the Order of Malta, were studying hard. The Marquise was always pleased to tell their father when they won prizes. As for Madeleine-Laure, aged ten, she still could not write, and she was very quarrelsome.

Her mother also had difficulty in writing because like her husband she suffered badly from haemorrhoids and could not always sit down to compose a letter. Neither could she walk, and so she could not go out. Her maid and La Jeunesse looked after her well, but the inflammation was so bad that she was given applications of leeches. The doctors of the eighteenth century, like their successors in the nineteenth, did not know how to deal with this problem. As soon as possible, however, the Marquise resumed her shopping trips and on 31 January 1781 she was able to send a new kind of luxury to the prisoner whose detention deprived him of his garden at La Coste. She sent 'three dozen flower bulbs, three tuberoses and three jonquils (they are labelled)'. His cell was not lacking in comfort.

At the end of December 1783 Louis-Marie de Sade had informed his father that he was about to join a new infantry regiment, the Rohan-Soubise, and the boy looked forward to his army career. The Marquis, however, was furious, because he wanted his son to join only Les Carabiniers de Monsieur, the regiment of the Comte de Provence, in which he had served as a young man. He no doubt knew that Renée-Pélagie's brother was in the army and possibly behind this choice but she, in order to stop him from accusing her of a Montreuil plot, told him that it was the King himself who wanted Louis-Marie to join the Rohan-Soubise.

There was more bad news from La Coste: on 25 January 1784, shortly after her fortieth birthday, Marie-Dorothée de Rousset died. Again, Renée-Pélagie did not show much obvious emotion. She reminded Gaufridy that her late friend had not paid for her stock of firewood, and she now wanted it taken back, it was *her* property. She also queried the wills her friend had made while asking for inventories of anything from the château she had used. It is undeniable that the Marquise tried to be so practical that she could easily become petty. Unfortunately too Gaufridy now saw all the letters she had written to Marie-Dorothée from Paris, and he was upset by unkind references to himself which questioned his honesty. Renée-Pélagie had to explain it all away.

The epistolary dialogue between Paris and Vincennes was briefly interrupted on 29 February 1784 when the prisoner suddenly found himself removed from his cell at nine o'clock in the evening. He was not being released, he was being taken to the Bastille, since the authorities, for unknown reasons, had decided to close Vincennes. (At the end of the twentieth century it is still there.) The Bastille itself, which contained only a very few other prisoners, had been scheduled for demolition, but nobody knew this and the public still saw the ancient and forbidding edifice as the symbol of despotic tyranny. Sade had not been allowed to take anything with him and after a week begged his wife to equip him. He described himself as 'naked'. He had to wait until the end of April before his possessions were sent on to him from Vincennes.

Fortunately his books and manuscripts followed him safely, for now, after twelve years in detention, he had channelled most, if not all, his energy into his writing. His wife had made work possible for him – books, some obscure, many expensive, others 'dangerous', from the censor's point of view, the special paper, pens, ink, candles: she had spent her days obtaining them for him, and nobody helped her financially. She was no doubt grateful that he was employing his time creatively, and if she still expressed her undying love she reminded him as often as she could that he must improve his behaviour or he would regret it for ever. When he behaved well she could see him often, and during the winter at least she could bring in 'secret' letters, concealed in her muff.

He was not her only problem. No sooner had her sons become young adults than they began to run up debts. She had to arrange for these to be paid, but she issued warnings that this situation must not continue. No doubt she realized the boys took after their father, but no young officer at the time made any serious attempt to avoid debt. Living beyond your means was customary if you happened to have been born an aristocrat.

Renée-Pélagie herself knew all about economy, but on the whole she was not much more sensible about money than her husband. Marie-Dorothée had once said that the two of them together were no more intelligent about money than a schoolboy. Yet the Marquise had a strong feeling in some ways about family duty, so strong that when her younger sister Françoise-Pélagie married the Marquis de Wavrin in 1783 she gave her a wedding present she could not afford and as a result increased her own difficulties.

In September 1784 Renée-Pélagie wrote a somewhat angry letter to Gaufridy 'because I am obliged to change my apartment because mine is being taken to be turned into cells'. However, she would stay in the convent because it would cost money to move and she would take what was given to her. The nuns realized that she would never complain, no doubt. 'It's a niche in an attic and yet we have three châteaux falling into decay because nobody lives in them.' Mazan and Saumane were in no better shape than La Coste, apparently. Gaufridy was to tell no one of the change, 'because my mother wanted me to take a more expensive [place]. Apart from the economy this house pleases me because I am alone ... I receive other people in the *parloir*. It is annoying, but I would tolerate such a thing ten thousand times over if I received justice on behalf of my husband'.

Two months later someone who had caused trouble in the past died at the age of forty – la Beauvoisin. She had done well for herself. The sale of her effects, which included two hundred rings, unmounted diamonds and eighty dresses, caused a stir in Paris, even among ladies of quality. Sade had been fascinated by her, and she, apparently, by him, but he had returned to Renée-Pélagie, who was not interested in elegance or jewellery. She was the wife who had sold the few diamonds she possessed years before in order to visit her husband in prison near Lyon.

Late that same year the prisoner wrote her an extraordinary letter (not published until 1950, and referred to as *La vanille et la manille*), background to his need for *flacons* and *étuis*. It explains the difficulty he experienced in achieving orgasm, even when he had a partner, and after Réne-Pélagie had read it there was nothing she did not know about his masturbatory activities. He also reminded her that she had seen something of these problems at La Coste, evidence that she was not necessarily as naïve about his sexual problems and demands as might have appeared when she was first asked to order the *flacons* and *étuis*.

The Marquise had recently had to deal with the loss of her sister, her friend and her former housekeeper. Now, in 1785, came the illness and death of La Jeunesse. Renée-Pélagie had nursed him herself, but could not save him. She mentioned in a letter to Gaufridy that the valet's illness had cost her a good deal of money, but she did not seem to regret it, presumably because the man had been so close to her husband for a very long time, had copied his manuscripts and also helped her. He had been so valuable that she had even forgiven his frequent absences when he went out drinking. She sold his clothes and sent the pitiful sum of money they earned to the wife and children he had abandoned years before in Langres.

She still provided the prisoner in the Bastille with eau-de-Cologne and wine, asked the governor to allow him exercise, continuing the work of the last twelve years, and told him society bored her; she thought only of him. 'We shall live and die together,' she wrote. 'I build a thousand castles in Spain for the moment of your release.' Yet she seemed all the same to be slightly more distant. She was by now possibly affected to some extent by the convent atmosphere in which she lived. In February 1787 she actually suggested to her husband that he should see the confessor who was available to the Bastille prisoners, a certain Abbé Duquesne. She told him that he was an intelligent man 'with whom one can discuss literature', and this would be one other person to see. She also found the courage to write to him about the piety which had irritated him so much in the past. He did not understand what piety, *la dévotion*, was: 'True piety is neither unsociable nor gloomy, you will see. For I shall not give up my religious duties when you come out, since one of religion's essential duties is to contribute to the happiness of all those who surround us.' She reassured him: 'So, you can see that my duty is allied to the inclination of my heart, you have nothing to fear.'

She also told him that God accepted only true devotion and belief; he could see through any hypocrisy.

Her husband was nothing if not unpredictable. He was suddenly and deeply impressed by the popular sermons of Jean-Baptiste Massillon (1663–1742). He enthused to his wife about them, and the technique probably helped him with the counter-sermons he was to deliver in all his major works. Renée-Pélagie may in the past have seemed negligent of Christian duties but she never shared his atheism. She obtained for him a book with the intriguing title of *Le déisme réfuté par lui-même*, but she still found the courage to write to him about moral and spiritual problems, making it clear how she would behave when he was free: 'I shall not persecute you about adopting my way of thinking, although I do not and shall not cease to pray for that, because a forced and hypocritical homage cannot please God.'

Yet she still received those destructive letters which hurt her deeply and, as she pointed out, they could give him only a moment's satisfaction which would be followed by 'an eternity of regrets'. However, she tried to find the consolation of philosophy by stating that 'The satisfaction one feels through insulting a person clearly proves that they exist.' If she herself had started to exist, after long years of submission, the prisoner in one way had ceased to do so, for he had been absent from the world for ten years, and a family council was called to consider the legal situation. Naturally the Marquis asked for his freedom, saying he could then direct his own affairs, and just as naturally he was overruled through an understanding between the aged head of the family, the Commandeur de Sade, and the ever-active Madame de Montreuil. In June 1787 the Châtelet court in Paris confirmed that the Marquise now had official control of her children and of the Sade property. It is hardly surprising that her mother, in a letter to the lawyer, noted that her daughter appeared 'very calm', but she did not know if this was due to her having thought things over or whether she was being diplomatic towards the Commandeur and other senior members of the family. It was surely due to the fact that Renée-Pélagie foresaw at last some prospect of financial independence, realizing, as women have done ever since, that she was indeed helpless without it.

During the same month the Marquise received from her unpredictable husband expressions of concern about her health, forbidding her to walk in the streets, for they were dangerous and dirty, and if he knew she had arrived at the prison on foot he would refuse to see her. He even blamed her mother for allowing her to walk so much. But she could not afford carriages and how else would she have carried out all his requests unless she could walk about the city? He was writing incessantly but suffering from serious eye trouble, which did not preserve her from instructions to write better letters. He begged her to brighten up her style a little – 'the most monotonous things can be described with gaiety'. In August the previous year, after she had sent him a miniature of herself framed in tortoise-shell, she received what amounted to a declaration of love. It was impossible for him to express the pleasure he felt, this gift was 'delightful', 'divine', he embraced her and would thank her much better when he could clasp her in his arms. Everything about the portrait and frame pleased him – 'you would take away my life rather than an object which will stay with me until my death'.

Did Renée-Pélagie shed tears of pleasure or did she see what may have been true: were these not the words of a playwright, an actor, who could assume any role he chose and play it effectively in front of the ready-made audience of one who had been there for over twenty years? And she was ready, at least until now, to applaud him, whatever he did, said or wrote. Over these years she had taken little notice of outside events, she was too preoccupied with personal affairs, but gradually even she became aware that they were beginning to affect her life. In 1783, for instance, she noted that the war was over; the American War of Independence, which France had entered in 1778, had ended with the Treaty of Versailles; she had read this good news in *Le Mercure de France*. This 'official' news-sheet was sent to her from Provence and she told Gaufridy that if the next issue contained a denial of this, 'instead of sending it to me, please burn it!' As a mother with two sons in training for the forces she obviously did not want any more war.

Nor in principle did France, for the country had not made up for the losses sustained in the Seven Years War. Most of her overseas empire had now gone, as mentioned earlier, and there had been naval defeats as far apart as Brittany and West Africa. A succession of ministers attempted to right the financial situation, but superficial reforms were useless. The national treasury was empty for two basic and interlinked reasons: there were too many privileged people who could legally avoid paying most taxes, and the same privileged people understandably would not listen to any talk of change in the social structure.

This structure had been in place a long time and seemed impregnable. There were in France three 'Estates' or classes, the first consisting of the clergy, themselves great landowners who were exempted from paying tax. They could if they wished make gifts of money to the State, but their attitude was extremely selfish and they paid an infinitesimally small amount. The members of the Second Estate, the aristocrats, who were also privileged, consisted of three different groups. The first of these, the old nobility, the *noblesse d'épée*, included many people related to the royal family. The Sade family belonged to this group, while, as noted before, the Montreuils belonged to the second group, the *noblesse de robe*, which included many successful professional men, particularly those who practised law and had power in the courts. The third group was made up of 'nobles' who had simply bought their titles. Lastly there was the Third Estate, which included many members of the middle class who had often become rich and successful. However, they had a grievance, for they had no privileges and could take no part in the administration of the country. An important section of this Third Estate consisted of craftsmen, labourers, servants and peasants, many of these remaining very poor and, because they lacked any privileges, they could not avoid heavy taxes. The unfairness of this structure is only too clear.

Government ministers came and went, all of them trying to introduce reforms which would bring in more money to the state, but none of the privileged classes would accept anything that appeared to undermine their status. There was a growing atmosphere of unease, leading to riots in Brittany and the Dauphiné. At the same time the Government made various attempts to improve the situation by incorporating Lorraine in France and by making what they saw as a useful purchase: they bought the island of Corsica from the city state of Genoa, two weeks, as it happened, before the birth of Napoleon Bonaparte. Eventually, by August 1788, it was clear that the state of the country could be helped only by what were seen as desperate measures. It was decided to call a meeting of the States-General, all of the three estates. This had not happened for 175 years, but the King's words sounded hopeful: 'We need an assembly of our faithful subjects to help us get over all the difficulties in which we find ourselves with regard to our finances.'

The Estates were to assemble 'not only so that they may give their advice on everything we shall ask them to discuss, but also so that they may tell us the wishes and grievances of our people so that every kind of abuse will be reformed'.

This sounded like a call to democracy, but the King's advisers had left it too late. The harvest had failed in 1788, and the price of bread accordingly rose too high. The poor people could not afford to buy it and gradually the ideas of the *philosophes* found more converts. The meeting of the States-General did not take place until May 1789 and by then the Third Estate, which had been joined in the meantime by various members of the clergy and the nobility, had grown restive. They decided to call themselves the National Assembly, then the Constituent Assembly, intent on drafting a new constitution and refusing to obey the King. The revolutionary spirit spread quickly and on 14 July the Bastille, long regarded as the symbol of absolute monarchy, fell.

These last events, however, anticipate somewhat various developments in the story of Renée-Pélagie. In 1785 she had been forced to notice that a different atmosphere was pervading Paris, for she found herself prevented from seeing her husband. This, for once, was due not to his bad behaviour in the prison but to the scandal known as the 'affair of the diamond necklace'. The Cardinal de Rohan, who had once been ambassador to the court in Vienna, had lost the favour of the Queen, and he was so anxious to recover it that he allowed himself to be duped by an adventuress calling herself the Comtesse de la Motte. She persuaded him to obtain, ostensibly for the Queen, a valuable diamond necklace. He need not pay for it, the Queen would do that. The so-called Comtesse took the necklace, about which the Queen knew nothing, then had it broken up and sold. She and the Cardinal were arrested and tried. He was eventually acquitted, but banished from the court; she was flogged, branded and sentenced to life imprisonment. If she escaped and fled to England, the name of the Queen herself had been invoked in this miserable scandal and since she was already unpopular the people of Paris and of France in general did not forget the incident. Someone else did not forget it: Napoleon Bonaparte. Aged sixteen at the time, he had just been commissioned as a second lieutenant in the artillery and was already more than critical of the royal family. Later, with hindsight, he regarded this scandal as the start of the Revolution.

For a time the Cardinal de Rohan was imprisoned in the Bastille, which meant that all visits to detainees were forbidden. Renée-Pélagie naturally continued to write to her husband, her letters were usually short, and many, because of the prison rules, had to be addressed to the governor or his staff. She often wrote like a mother arranging care for a child or an invalid: could there be someone available near her husband to help him generally, since he was now so fat he could not even change his shirt on his own? Early in 1789 she passed on a request to Gaufridy: could he please arrange to send some truffles dressed in oil; the Marquis liked to eat them like that.

However, the prisoner, if he sometimes thanked her, continued to irritate her by giving her, in secret, letters more upsetting than ever, for he accused her of refusing to see or listen to him.

He was not her only correspondent. Gaufridy in many ways was still her confidant; there were no women she could write to now. While her husband was writing day and night and complained about her style, he did not see the reports she sent to Provence about events in Paris. She enjoyed describing melodramatic events – the fire at the Opéra in 1781 and the one at the Hôtel des Menus Plaisirs in April 1788. She had even developed a kind of staccato journalistic style. Six months later, however, she had other preoccupations and continued financial worries. She had heard that the Dauphin was so ill that he would surely die, and as a member of the aristocracy she realized that she would have to go into mourning for six months. But she had nothing to wear. 'I need black clothes,' she wrote to Gaufridy; 'mine are quite worn out and my daughter has none at all. However much the carriage will cost me it will be less expensive than buying something new.' Would he at once have her dresses packed, black and coloured, and even her linen, plus 'a kind of bed sheet trimmed with muslin at the length of a petticoat, if it has not been taken'. She realized that La Coste was being gradually emptied of anything of value. It was twenty-six years since she had left it.

The Dauphin died on 14 June 1789, when most people in France had other preoccupations.

When Renée-Pélagie visited the detainee in December 1788 he gave her a 'secret' letter that was more upsetting than ever and on the 29th she replied to it. Her husband had accused her of refusing to see him or listen to what he had to say. She was convinced he did not mean what he wrote 'or you are the most unjust of men'. She had done everything he asked with the papers he had given her, some sealed, some not. He knew she could hide nothing from him and believed that this was the reason why she was told nothing about his future. The tone of these letters is sombre, and she warned him that when he came out he would deeply regret his suspicions about her. He seems to have hinted that she was doing nothing to help him, that she was his enemy. In fact, her warning was deeply serious.

Within the next few months, if her feelings about her husband were changing, she found time to write a long report on the book the Marquis had just completed, his most intriguing, wide-ranging, non-pornographic work: *Aline et Valcour*. She herself had supplied him with all the background books he had needed in order to write it – travel books such as *Les voyages de Bougainville* and Captain Cook's accounts of his explorations. She had also tried to answer his questions about the topography of Spain and Portugal. Her letters to her husband may seem for the most part mundane and maternal, suffering by comparison with the thunder and lightning of his replies, yet her report on the novel is adult, straightforward, cool-headed yet personal. Parts of the manuscript made her cry, she said, and then she set out the principles by which one should judge 'a work which is a product of the mind'. One must agree in the first place about what is true: '. . . that which satisfies the general public most and contributes to the happiness of the total mass of people'. She discussed every aspect of the plot and ideas in the novel, although she had not yet read all of it.

Her report, incomplete though it is, includes her own views on all the themes Sade was writing about – from sodomy, the problem of punishment, the wish to dethrone the sovereign, to man's treatment of animals, to list merely a few. She found most aspects of the book, if not all, well executed and allowed herself to offer some advice: for instance, prison reform (a subject of concern to both writer and reader) must be gradual and the praise of the English should be better handled. She added that she was writing 'only what comes into my mind through what I read'. The Age of Reason, along with its great authors, was coming to an end. Both Voltaire and Rousseau had died in 1778, D'Alembert in 1783, Diderot a year later. A new generation, including Chateaubriand and Madame de Staël, was growing up while Sade, using eighteenth-century techniques and anarchic ideas, thanks to his detention and his wife, was producing a body of work unique in Europe. Renée-Pélagie was virtually the only person to have read any of it.

Aline et Valcour was published in 1795 and Sade was proud of it. Perhaps he remembered his helper on several occasions: when his heroine Aline attacked the system of arranged marriages and when, in a moment of calm and possessive complacency, he wrote: 'No, no, there is no woman in the world equal to the one who belongs to us. . . . She is at the same time our wife and our mistress, our sister and our god. . . .' She had certainly belonged to him, but for how much longer? Yet maybe the social climate was changing. Choderlos de Laclos, that same year, only three years after publishing his great novel *Les liaisons dangereuses*, began to write about the education of women; but it was too early to reach the public. In any case, *Aline et Valcour* is a richer remembrance of Renée-Pélagie than the unconscious contribution she made to the naïve and long-suffering Justine. Her work as author's assistant proves her to have been more intelligent than she might have appeared in all those hundreds of frustrated letters, but she had been trapped, like so many women of her century and after: she had not had enough education; her upbringing and her arranged marriage had taken her on a collision course with her mother and left her with a lifetime of shopping lists. No woman failed to respond to Sade, but Renée-Pélagie had taken on the hardest task of all: she had accepted him for better or worse, and it had been worst of all.

In her little attic room Renée-Pélagie probably read a good deal, especially since she was alone and could hardly walk. She had probably never thought about politics, she had no doubt assumed that the Bourbons would be monarchs for ever, and *Le Mercure de France* would not lead her to change her mind. The enterprising *Journal des dames*, which encouraged even women to think about social and political questions and might have appealed to Mademoiselle de Rousset, would be out of her range. Yet, she could not fail to notice the changed atmosphere in the city, and she kept Gaufridy up to date about the signs of discontent. She described the confused Réveillon riots in April 1789 and if, one month later, she thought it was all over, there were still soldiers everywhere and it was impossible to disentangle rumour from truth. 'What is upsetting,' she wrote, 'is the extreme wretchedness of the poor.' She had heard that many people had died through non-payment of debts and delays in the payment of small sums. She thought that everyone should be paid at least what they needed for bread, a simplistic but common-sense attitude, typical of Renée-Pélagie. However, although she gave Gaufridy other news of events in Paris, combined with depressing news of her own health, she did not tell him everything.

7 Solitary Mother

My taste is truly for solitude. – *Renée-Pélagie de Sade*

If Madame de Montreuil still employed spies in Paris she would have been one of the first to know what had happened to her son-in-law in early June 1789. Despite the omnipresent troops in Paris the movement towards revolution was gathering momentum, the States-General had met in May and Sade in the Bastille was well aware, mainly through his wife, of the unrest in the streets. As a born revolutionary he longed to be closer to the action and on 2 July he started shouting to the crowds through the window of his cell, using a funnel as a loud hailer. He did all he could to heighten the tension, saying that prisoners were being murdered. There were in fact only seven or eight men in the Bastille, but by 4 July there was one less, for the governor had decided to remove the tiresome Monsieur de Sade. Six men, armed with pistols, dragged him from his bed in the small hours, gave him no time to dress, pushed him into a fiacre and drove him to Charenton-Saint-Maurice, the hospice for the insane. He was not insane, merely seditious. He was not allowed to take anything with him. His cell was sealed and his wife was later authorized to remove all his possessions.

Renée-Pélagie, however, had gone temporarily into the country, for, as she told Gaufridy later, 'the revolution which has just started and is not yet over calms neither the heart nor the mind'. She had intended to come to the Bastille, with the police commissioner responsible, one Chenon, but unfortunately she chose the wrong day, 14 July. Chenon was called away to deal with trouble elsewhere and apparently the visit was postponed. The seven prisoners left in the Bastille were released, the governor was murdered and his head paraded through the streets on a pike.

Five days later, Renée-Pélagie, as though exhausted by the combined problems of her husband and the dangerous chaos of the Revolution, decided she had had enough. She told Chenon that she no longer wished to be responsible for the Marquis's possessions. He could dispose of them more or less as he thought fit. She added that she had 'personal reasons' for her decision. Her main reason no doubt was that suddenly, or perhaps not even suddenly, she could not tolerate the thought of living with her husband again. She was ready for separation.

By the end of the month it was too late for Sade. His cell had been ransacked, everything had gone. His reaction was understandable, he wept 'tears of blood' at the loss of his valuable library and his even more valuable manuscripts. He fulminated against his wife's failure – her 'treason', he called it. He had consoled himself that he had not wasted his time in prison, maybe his writings could have earned him some money, all hope of which had now vanished. 'Madame de Sade dined, went to the *garde-robe* [i.e. the W.C.], confessed and went to sleep.' Why had she done nothing for ten days: 'Oh! Madame de Sade, how your mind is changed!' It was more than he could bear, for furniture could be replaced, but not ideas. He had heard too that she had not even kept all the papers he had given her earlier. She had given some to other people, who had destroyed them.

There was no one explanation for her action or inaction. She had been in the country because she was frightened and aware that food was disappearing rapidly from the city. She had come back in order to claim some money but she had not slept for three nights. Unimaginable things had happened, she told Gaufridy: 'They have to be seen to be believed and our descendants will think they are exaggerated.' In September she wrote more graphic details.

She saw the whole thing as 'a river in flood or a watch where the mainspring is broken. All the reasoning in the world, all calculations will not make it work; the mainspring has to be replaced.' She gave some explanation of her behaviour: 'I can truly see that I'm losing my memory, I'm exhausted after two years spent listening to everything I was told, thinking, reflecting, replying, making arrangements.' She had become tense with effort: she had had to avoid compromising herself; she could not trust anyone. She had decided to stay apart from politics and not read any of the pamphlets that were now on sale. She noticed, however, that 'The poor are becoming very numerous', business was bad, taxes were not paid. 'All this is too overwhelming to last; disorder has reached the point when it will bring back order.' In the middle of this letter she had written 'Monsieur de Sade is well', and she remained dutiful in one way, although obviously thinking of her children's future. Having heard that there was likely to be trouble in Provence, she asked the lawyer to safeguard all the essential papers relating to La Coste and the Sade family. Nobody except very trustworthy people were to know their hiding-place and this must also be somewhere safe from rats.

She had been totally destabilized by events, but for some time her attitude towards her husband had changed, partly because her health had deteriorated so rapidly but principally no doubt because she could not stand his accusations and complaints any longer. From time to time he had skilfully expressed affection, remembering her fête-day for instance, just as she had made an emotional reference to their wedding anniversary, but how often did he really mean what he said? He told Gaufridy later that he had noticed her changed attitude, blaming her confessor's attempts to restore her to total piety, but he also knew very well that he needed her, and therefore had said nothing. He had even apologized for asking for money when she was ill. Perhaps he hoped that her mood would change, but there was still no mention, however remote, of his release, and after all, 'hope deferred maketh the heart sick'. It is not clear at what point he learnt the unexpected news, that she wanted a separation, or why, but he probably did not hear about this until later.

Renée-Pélagie continued to write to Gaufridy with graphic accounts of what was happening in Paris and how difficult it was to buy anything, for nobody could find any cash any more. On 23 March 1790 the lawyer received other information, this time from Madame de Montreuil. On the 20th, as he surely knew, the National Assembly had issued a decree abolishing the system of *lettres de cachet*, and there were various ways in which the family of a detainee could handle the situation. She seemed to favour a course of inaction. Her daughter, however, was taking action in a different way. She wrote to Gaufridy on 2 April, saying she had just time to tell him that 'Monsieur de Sade was freed on Good Friday, which was yesterday. He wants to see me, but I have replied that I still planned to separate, it cannot be otherwise.' She asked for her effects and papers to be sent to her mother's address. She had told the Marquis that when he wanted money he was to write to Gaufridy, who was acting on his behalf. She added, meaningfully: 'He will certainly write to you.' He did so ten days later, and continued to do so for years to come.

Money: the letters and legal documents about money accumulated on all sides. The Marquis had hoped to receive money through legacies from various relatives, but gave up in the end. He realized he would never receive anything. He accused his wife of having kept the money he should have inherited from his mother, the Dowager Comtesse, but this situation remains obscure. If she had kept the money, she would have spent it on him, for *lettre de cachet* detainees were kept by their families not by the State. He knew he would have to repay the dowry which he had received in 1763 and mostly spent, but despite complex arrangements Renée-Pélagie never received her due. She steadfastly refused to see her husband.

The Marquise must have planned her petition for separation much earlier, for by 9 June 1790 it was granted by the court of the Châtelet. She had stated in advance that her husband would know deep in his heart why she could do nothing else. In order to justify herself she intended to say 'only what he will force me to say. But I shall say it if he forces me to do so'. Sade of course was not given to feeling guilty or blaming himself, and it was easy enough for him to blame his in-laws, especially Madame de Montreuil, for everything that had gone wrong in his life. It was impossible to escape her. She had waited patiently for her daughter to return to her, and in one way it was fortunate for Sade that she was still there, for he even borrowed money from her. Perhaps he hoped that his poverty on leaving Charenton might make her feel guilty.

In the meantime how had Renée-Pélagie been living, and what was her future? Although she had noticed the poverty of working people, she was not the sort of woman to join in their struggle. She was no *frondeuse*. She had been very frightened, especially on 5 October the previous year: 'I fled from Paris with my daughter, a maid and no lackey,' she wrote in her usual hurried style, 'following the general tide in a hired carriage in order not to be dragged off by the working-class women who were forcibly taking all the women from the houses in order to get the King out of Versailles and making them go on foot in the rain and the dirt, etc.' She reached her destination, although she did not say where this was. 'The King is in Paris; he was led to the city, with the heads of two royal bodyguards on pikes in front, and from there to the Louvre. In Paris they are wild with joy because they think the presence of the King is going to produce bread.' She stayed in the country, not because she was afraid of being killed, but because she did not want to die of hunger and she had no money. The problems of money were endless, but at least she saw her elder son briefly, on leave from the army, and she tried to keep him with her.

Could women hope for anything from the Revolution? Had the march to Versailles led them into any feeling of solidarity? A very few women tried to make their voices heard: Olympe de Gouges, for instance, who was actually able to publish in 1791 her *Déclaration des droits de la femme et de la citoyenne*. Later she founded the Club des Tricoteuses, but in 1793 she went to the guillotine, for like so many early feminists she was confused and had foolishly spoken in defence of the King. She believed, like a few other feminists, that if women had the right to die on the scaffold then they should have the same right to speak in public.

There was also Théroigne de Méricourt, pretty when young and apparently admired by Sade after his release from Charenton in 1790. Known as *la belle Amazone*, she acquired some influence, but she became too moderate and at the end of March 1793 she was publicly flogged by working-class women who did not understand her ideas. She went mad and died in 1817.

Madame Roland, the former country girl who wrote charming memoirs while in prison, was guillotined in 1793 after her involvement with the Girondists. 'O liberty!' she said shortly before her death, 'what crimes are committed in thy name!' The same year brought the same fate to a very different woman: Madame du Barry, who was accused of having wasted the nation's money. The fate of Queen Marie-Antoinette, who followed her husband to the guillotine, is well known, while Charlotte Corday, born an aristocrat and descended from the great Corneille, was executed at the age of twenty-six after her murder of the later sanctified oppressor, Jean-Paul Marat. She was simple-minded enough to have been convinced that his death would profit the nation. It would be some time before women in France could make any effective contribution to the feminist cause, for the concept of solidarity was unknown to them, and it is worth noting that across the Channel Mary Wollstonecraft, who visited Paris during the Terror, referred later to the women's march to Versailles as 'strictly a mob'.

The Montreuils, as members of the *noblesse de robe*, were suspect to many of the new men who came to power during these desperate years. They had both spent some time in prison and might even have gone to the guillotine, but they were saved, ironically enough, by their son-in-law, who was now Citizen

Sade and had acquired some civic power. Seeing their name on a list of people whose fate had to be decided by his 'Section', he said nothing. When it came to a question of life or death, no thought of revenge occurred to him. Did he remember the Christian admonishment to love your enemy? Did he remember the few happy times in their long association? They had after all brought up his two sons, whom he now saw occasionally. And for years their daughter had been his *chère amie*, and what would he have done without her?

However, Renée-Pélagie had been instantly replaced by a younger woman who in some ways behaved as she had done. Marie-Constance Quesnet was a deserted wife with a young son. She devoted herself to Sade from late August 1790 until his death in 1814. She was more actively enterprising than Renée-Pélagie, for she later tried to sell his plays for him, but of course her predecessor had helped indirectly in the writing of them. Like la Beauvoisin earlier she was even ready to give up her house to help the Marquis. He called her *Sensible*, Sensitive, and claimed their relationship was platonic. Renée-Pélagie would certainly have known about her existence, for the Sade sons, when they were in Paris, saw both parents. Marie-Constance had once been a professional actress, apparently, and with Sade, the perpetual actor, an extraordinary scheme was launched: 'Sensible', with the help of a mediator, would meet Renée-Pélagie and convince her of the Marquis's dire poverty. Surely she would do something to help him? But Louis-Marie put a stop to this suggestion. He no doubt saw how much it would upset his mother.

Her two sons, and God, provided comfort for Renée-Pélagie. Nobody needed her now. Her father had died in 1794, her mother four years later, aged seventy-eight. Renée-Pélagie now spent as much time as she could at Echauffour, gradually going blind and forced to spend her days in an invalid's chair. The Montreuils had been respected in the area and as a result the château was not attacked by the revolutionaries. Nevertheless, the local church of Saint-André was less fortunate. It was used as a saltpetre store and as an abattoir, while the presbytery was sold.

La Coste did not escape; the Revolution brought changes of

many sorts. The château had housed the village prison beneath the lived-in areas, but this was now abandoned, and in any case much of the near-feudal administration had faded out before it was officially abolished in August 1789. In 1792 the half-empty building was pillaged, although the villagers managed to save some effects. Four years later the Marquis succeeded in selling what remained of it – a sale that developed into another hard-to-believe drama, outside the scope of this story. The Marquise was supposed to receive some money from the transaction, but she didn't.

In the meantime, how much did she know of what was happening to her husband? If she had not suddenly broken away and remained with him as she had vowed to do ever since 1777, what sort of life would they have lived together? Would they have disappeared from Paris and lived quietly in Provence or Normandy? What they would have lived on is obscure. Renée-Pélagie told Gaufridy later that she had emigrated, although she did not say where. Both her sons went abroad, and since emigration had been decreed a capital offence, their father was angry and, writing to their mother, tried to force them to return. It so happened that the Marquis, calling himself Citizen Sade, was the only member of the family who did not emigrate, although he was suspected of wanting to do so. It is indeed hard to assess how this couple, so long separated by his detention, might have lived, but Sade, despite his new companion, 'Sensible', and his determination to become a writer, lived for a time a wandering, penniless existence full of contrasts which reflected closely the destabilization of the period. Soon after leaving Charenton he was received by the Comte de Clermont-Tonnerre, a cousin by marriage, but in 1794 this cousin was thrown out of a window and killed. Sade, who believed in monarchy, provided it was controlled by a body such as the English Parliament, did not know if he was an aristocrat or a democrat: he was so confused that he even asked Gaufridy to tell him. His predicament and confusion mirrored the problems of many members of the former First and Second Estates.

Renée-Pélagie, if she had chosen to stay with her husband, could surely not have faced his penniless existence, and even her parents, as members of the *noblesse de robe*, were in trouble. There were some dramatic moments in Sade's poverty-stricken life: he was reduced to stealing property from his elder son's apartment in order to sell it for food. He even worked in a theatre at Versailles, for miserable pay, and if he was pleased to act a part in his own play *Oxtiern*, the performance was hardly a success. Some of his books were published, but the author usually remained anonymous and did not earn much from them. Instead he earned the attention of the authorities and in 1801 was sent to prison for his 'obscene' writings. The Consulate, and especially the First Consul, Bonaparte, reacted strongly against any work considered licentious: it prolonged the atmosphere of the *ancien régime*. Sade was in worse trouble still, for while in the prison of Sainte-Pélagie he was accused of trying to seduce young male prisoners and was sent to Bicêtre, a low-class mental hospital-cum-prison. From there he was sent in 1803 to Charenton, where he had been before and where he remained until his death.

By now Renée-Pélagie, who may have heard something about her former husband's precarious life, had grown older and her three children had grown up. If her daughter Madeleine-Laure was not interested in marriage, having devoted herself to her mother and the religious life, her two brothers, when the Revolution was over, were both ready to look for brides. But this was not easy, and if Louis-Marie, calling himself Sade de Mazan, was well received in some sections of Parisian society, he still had to live down the early legend of his father. One young woman, who later became Madame de Chastenay, liked the young man but could not face the prospect of bearing grand-children of the Marquis de Sade. Claude-Armand made what appeared to be a clever choice: he had met a woman of thirty-six who belonged to one of the other branches of the family, Louise-Gabrielle-Laure de Sade d'Eyguières, and determined to marry her. His father was pleased that the two families would thus be united, but Louis-Marie tried to sabotage the plan by saying that it was a trap, his father might well be removed from Charenton and sent to a secure prison. In the end Claude-Armand was successful. He married Laure at Condé-en-Brie in 1808, and they had several children, including Alphonse-Ignace, who inherited the family title on his father's death in 1847. One of Claude-Armand's daughters, Laure Émilie, married Gaston de Menildurand in 1839 and the Château d'Echauffour is today owned by their great-grandson, General (Vicomte) Pierre Lesquen du Plessis Casso.

Sadly, in 1809, Louis-Marie, his father's favourite, who had studied botanical illustration and written a *Histoire de la nation française* was killed in a military skirmish in Italy. His father was sorry that Renée-Pélagie was told this tragic news, which could not have helped her. She herself died on 7 July 1810. Her husband is said to have wept at the loss of his former *chère amie*. Their daughter remained at Echauffour until her death in 1844, spending the rest of her life in pious devotion.

Did the Marquise, in her Normandy château, pray for her separated husband, whose 'crimes' she had always forgiven? Had she read anything he had written beyond his plays and *Aline et Valcour*? How much did she hear about *Justine*, *La nouvelle Justine*, *Juliette*, *La philosophie dans le boudoir*, *Les crimes de l'amour*, even if the first four were published anonymously? She would surely not have forgotten the so-called 'orgies' at the Château de La Coste, but she would not have been reminded of them by the stories of the Château de Silling, for the manuscript of *Les 120 journées de Sodome* had remained hidden in the walls of the Bastille until it was found, kept in private hands for decades and not published until 1904. She no doubt heard too about the Marquis's imprisonment in 1801 for obscene writing.

She had been no less institutionalized than her husband, for after his years in Vincennes and the Bastille he felt he would become a Trappist, which he didn't, but she in her way did so. She retreated from the imprisonment of her irrational relationship and escaped into the silence of her solitude. She was probably frightened of what would have been a new and different relationship if Sade were released from Charenton, but she was not frightened of her new independence.

There was a curious symbolism in the whole story, so many missing elements that can be restored only through the imagination. As noted earlier, no authentic portrait of Renée-Pélagie has survived. The one that has sometimes been said to represent her is considered more likely to show her mother-in-law, the Comtesse, and we do not know what she looked like. The same is true of her mysterious sister, who may have been the romantic love of Sade's life. Her portrait was found in Sade's room at Charenton after his death, but then vanished. What happened to those vital *petits papiers* for which Madame de Montreuil searched so obstinately? When the little red chest that was supposed to contain them eventually reached Paris from La Coste, it was found to be empty.

The lawyer Gaufridy sent many things from the château and included, no doubt by mistake, some of the costumes that had once been used in comedy theatricals at the château. The whole of this story was in its way a tragicomedy, a moral tale, and for many years an epistolary novel, all in the eighteenth-century tradition. There were no costumes for Renée-Pélagie. She had no doubt received and worn the old mourning wear she had asked for in 1788, and after 1789 mourning was her lot. Both partners had been aware of the powerful presence that could be established by clothes. She had sent him, at his request, the sleeve of a dress she had worn, and he asked her to send him an embroidered jacket saying she must embroider it herself, otherwise he would send it back. *Ma Pénélope*, he once called her, even after the separation. Perhaps only those who have been truly close could become as far apart as they then became.

Renée-Pélagie was a deeply feminine woman. It was hard for her, in the context of her century, to achieve independence. She did not work, she was untrained in anything beyond family administration, but without any help, except possibly from God, she learnt to be herself. For a woman married off at twenty-one to a uniquely wayward man, imprisoned all her life emotionally and financially by her authoritarian mother, this itself was an achievement. She occupies a small but crucial place in the history of feminism, for Sade, regarded by those who do not really know him as the most dangerously macho writer who ever existed, would surely not have written his major works if she had not been there. Those who have studied his life and work know that women in one way or another controlled his destiny and that he himself was continually fascinated by their varied existence and the power they possessed. Women of one sort or another, from la Beauvoisin to Marie-Dorothée de Rousset, from Anne-Prospère to Gothon, moved in and out of his life, but Renée-Pélagie was constantly there from 1763 to 1790, nearly thirty years, constantly needed.

Without her their younger son Claude-Armand would not have existed and there would have been no member of the family to visit the Marquis as he lay dying in Charenton. It was to be expected that she and her parents would have brought up the children in the Christian tradition, but this surviving son turned into a prude. It has to be remembered that after the licentious decades of the eighteenth century and its intensely erotic productions in literature and art, a reaction set in and censorship under the Directory and the Consulate became severe. Claude-Armand, unloved by his father's biographers and literary analysts, had many Sade manuscripts destroyed and tried hard to remove any details of Sade authorship from the reference books of the time.

Yet his mother had earned and retained his affection. After her death he gave money to the church of Saint-André at Echauffour so that masses could be said for her. He also gave a lamp, which was to be lit on religious fête-days in her memory. Sadly, like so much of her story, it has disappeared. But she is not forgotten. In the cemetery at Echauffour it is still possible to read her epitaph, which commemorates her good works. Her true immortality is in the unquestioning love she gave to her husband for so long, which surely saved his reason, for she was the only one who listened to him and tried to understand him. Was she right to forgive him so much? The question remains unresolved, but it is one that will always be meaningful to women.

Chronology
and Historical Background

1740	Birth in Paris of Donatien-Alphonse-François de Sade, 2 June.
1741	Birth of Renée-Pélagie de Montreuil, 2 December.
1756	Outbreak of the Seven Years War
1759	Sade becomes a captain in the cavalry regiment of Bourgogne.
1762	Publication of *Du contrat social* and *Émile* by Rousseau.
1763	Sade is demobilized at the end of the Seven Years War. Marriage of Renée-Pélagie de Montreuil to the Marquis de Sade in Paris, 17 May. Sade imprisoned briefly in Vincennes (29 October) for beating Jeanne Testard, with impiety. Released on condition he stays for some months at the Montreuil Château d'Echauffour in Normandy.
1764	Death of Madame de Pompadour, *maîtresse en titre* to King Louis XV. Dissolution in France of the Society of Jesus.
1764–6	Sade has liaisons with various actresses and takes

one of them, Mademoiselle de Beauvoisin, to his Château de La Coste, allegedly presenting her as the Marquise.

1767   Death of the Comte de Sade, 24 January. Birth of Louis-Marie, first son of the Marquis and Marquise de Sade, 27 August.

1768   Imprisonment of the Marquis de Sade in Saumur for the flagellation of Rose Keller, 3 April. On his transfer to Pierre-Encise, near Lyon, the Marquise sells her diamonds in order to visit him. He is released on 16 November.

1769   Birth of second son of the Marquis and Marquise de Sade, Donatien-Claude-Armand, 27 June. Birth of Napoleon Bonaparte in Corsica.

1770   The Dauphin of France, grandson of Louis XV, marries Princess Marie-Antoinette of Austria.

1771   Birth of third child of the Marquis and Marquise de Sade, Madeleine-Laure, 17 April.

1771?–2   Liaison between Renée-Pélagie's sister, Anne-Prospère, and the Marquis de Sade.

1772   The 'poisoned sweets' affair in Marseille, 23 June. Sade flees to Italy, followed by Anne-Prospère. He is sentenced to death *in absentia*, on charges of poisoning and sodomy. Arrested at Chambéry, imprisoned at Miolans, where his wife attempts unsuccessfully to visit him.

1773   Sade escapes from prison and returns to the Château de La Coste.

1774   Raid on the Château de La Coste, ordered by Madame de Montreuil, 6 January. Sade, forewarned, is not captured. Renée-Pélagie attempts legal action against her mother for interference in her family affairs. Death of Louis XV. Accession of his grandson, Louis XVI, aged twenty. Renée-Pélagie meets Sade in Lyon.

1775   Sexual orgies at La Coste with young servants engaged for the purpose. Renée-Pélagie is possibly implicated. In July Sade escapes to Italy a second time.

1776   Sade returns to La Coste in June.

1777   Further orgies at La Coste end with an attempt on Sade's life by the father of one girl, a participant. Renée-Pélagie and the girl travel to Paris, Sade travelling there separately. His mother was reported ill but she dies before he and his wife arrive. He is arrested at the Hôtel de Danemark, where his wife is staying, on 13 February, and imprisoned at Vincennes. Death of the Abbé de Sade, 31 December.

1778   France enters the American War of Independence. Sade authorized to travel to Aix, where the 1772 death sentence is quashed, although he is admonished for 'exaggerated debauchery'. Escapes on his way to Paris, returns to La Coste but is recaptured after a few weeks of liberty in August. His wife, in Paris, eventually learns that he is detained at Vincennes but is not allowed to visit him.

1779   Marie-Dorothée de Rousset stays with the Marquise de Sade in Paris.

1781   Death of Anne-Prospère de Launay, 13 May. Renée-Pélagie's first visit to her husband in prison, still detained by *lettre de cachet*, 13 July.

1782   Sade begins serious writing.

1783   American War of Independence is ended by the Treaty of Versailles.

1784   Beaumarchais's play *Le mariage de Figaro*, previously banned for three years by royal censorship for its derision of the *ancien régime*, is performed with success. Death of Marie-Dorothée de Rousset, 25 January. Sade is transferred to the Bastille.

1785   The 'affair of the diamond necklace', implicating the Cardinal de Rohan and Queen Marie-Antoinette, leads to a suspension of visits to prisoners in the Bastille.

1788   The King is advised to convoke the States-General. Failure of the harvest. Sade loses control of his affairs, while Renée-Pélagie gains some financial rights of her own.

1789   Riots in Rennes and Paris. The States-General meet in May. In June the Third Estate makes a bid for power by calling itself the National Assembly, and less than a month later the Bastille falls, on 14 July. In early July Sade is transferred to Charenton-Saint-Maurice, the hospice for the insane, after shouting to the mob outside the prison that fellow-prisoners are being murdered.

1790   The *lettre de cachet* system for imprisonment is cancelled, leading to Sade's release from Charenton on 2 April. Renée-Pélagie's request for legal separation is granted.

1791   First (anonymous) publication of Sade's writing: *Justine ou les malheurs de la vertu*. Death of Mirabeau. The royal family flee to Varennes.

1792   The Château de La Coste is vandalized in September. Just afterwards, on 22 September, the monarchy is abolished.

1793   Execution of Louis XVI, 21 January. Murder of Marat by Charlotte Corday, 13 July. Sade helps spare the life of Renée-Pélagie's parents by remaining silent when their names are added to a list of people meriting the guillotine. Accused of supporting the 'enemies of the Republic', Sade is arrested. Execution of Marie-Antoinette, 16 October.

1794   Sade sentenced to death but released after fall and execution of Robespierre.

1795	Start of the Directory. Death of the Président de Montreuil. Publication of *Aline et Valcour*.
1796	Sade sells La Coste.
1797	Anonymous publication of *La nouvelle Justine*, etc.
1798	Death of Madame de Montreuil.
1799	Sade works in the theatre for miserable pay and acts in his own play, *Oxtiern*. Bonaparte's *coup d'état*, 18 brumaire, followed by the Consulate.
1801	Sade imprisoned at Sainte-Pélagie for 'obscene' work, following an earlier seizure of *Justine* in a new edition.
1803	Sade is accused of trying to seduce male fellow-prisoners sent to the prison-asylum at Bicêtre and then to Charenton.
1804	Bonaparte crowns himself Emperor.
1808	Marriage of Claude-Armand de Sade.
1809	Death of Louis-Marie de Sade.
1810	Death of Renée-Pélagie, Marquise de Sade, at Echauffour, 7 July.
1814	Death of Sade, 2 December.
1815	Battle of Waterloo, followed by exile of Napoleon.
1844	Death of Madeleine-Laure de Sade.
1847	Death of Claude-Armand de Sade.

Bibliography

Sade's Writings

Le Marquis de Sade: *Oeuvres complètes du Marquis de Sade.* Edition mise en place par Annie Le Brun et J.-J. Pauvert. Paris: Pauvert, 1986–

——: *Lettres choisies.* Préface de Gilbert Lely. Paris: Pauvert, 1963

Bourdin, Paul (ed.): *Correspondance inédite du Marquis de Sade, de ses proches et de ses familiers.* Paris: Librairie de France, 1929

Daumas, Georges et Lely, Gilbert (eds): *Lettres et mélanges littéraires écrits à Vincennes et à la Bastille. Avec des lettres de Madame de Sade, de Marie-Dorothée de Rousset et de diverses personnes.* Paris: Borderie, 1980

Debauve, Jean-Louis (ed.): *Lettres inédites et documents retrouvés.* Paris: Ramsay/Pauvert, 1990

Lely, Gilbert (ed.): *L'aigle, mademoiselle . . . Lettres publieés pour la première fois sur les manuscrits autographes inédits avec une préface et un commentaire.* Paris: Georges Artigues, 1949

Biographies and Histories

Apollinaire, Guillaume: *Les diables amoureux.* Paris: Gallimard, 1964

Beauvoir, Simone de: *Le deuxième sexe.* Paris: Gallimard, 2 vols,

1949–50. Trans. as *The Second Sex* by H. M. Parshley. London: Cape, 1953

——: *Faut-il brûler Sade?* Paris: Gallimard, 1955

Carter, Angela: *The Sadeian Woman*. London: Virago, 1979

Cobban, Alfred: *A History of Modern France*. Harmondsworth, Middx: Penguin, Vol. 1, 3rd ed., 1963

Davis, N. Z. and Farge, Arlette (eds): *A History of Women in the West*, Vol. 3: *Renaissance and Englightenment Paradoxes*. Cambridge, Mass.: Harvard University Press, 1993

Delpech, Janine: *La passion de la Marquise de Sade*. Paris: Planète, 1970

Farr, Evelyn: *Before the Deluge: Parisian Society in the Reign of Louis XVI*. London: Peter Owen, 1994

Fauville, Henri: *La Coste: Sade en Provence*. Aix-en-Provence: Edisud, 1984

Gaxotte, Pierre: *Paris au 18ième siècle*. Paris: Arthaud, 1968

Ginisty, Paul: *La Marquise de Sade* (lead essay). Paris: Charpentier, 1901

Gorer, Geoffrey: *The Life and Ideas of the Marquis de Sade* (enlarged and revised ed.). London: Peter Owen, 1953

Hayman, Ronald: *De Sade: A Critical Biography*. London: Constable, 1978

Jean, Raymond: *Portrait de Sade*. Arles: Actes-Sud, 1989

Laborde, Alice: *Le mariage du Marquis de Sade*. Paris/Geneva: Champion-Slatkine, 1988

Lely, Gilbert: *Vie du Marquis du Sade*. Paris: Gallimard, 2 vols, 1952–7

Lesquen du Plessis Casso, General (Vicomte) Pierre de: *Histoire du Château d'Echauffour* (unpublished monograph). 1979

Lever, Maurice: *Marquis de Sade: A Biography*. London: Harper Collins, 1993

Mishima, Yukio, *Madame de Sade* (play). London: Peter Owen, 1968

Pauvert, Jean-Jacques: *Sade vivant*. Paris: Robert Laffont, 3 vols, 1986–90

Rosenthal, Miriam: *The French Revolution* (Then and There series). London: Longmans, 1965

Bibliography

Periodicals

Magazine littéraire, No. 284: 'Sade écrivain' (series of articles). Jan. 1991
Warwick Journal of Philosophy: The Divine Sade (includes Margaret Crosland, 'Madame de Sade and Other Problems'), 1994

Anthology

The Passionate Philosopher: A Marquis de Sade Reader. Selected and translated, with an Introduction by Margaret Crosland. London: Peter Owen, 1991

149

Index

Some multiple names and forenames are abbreviated

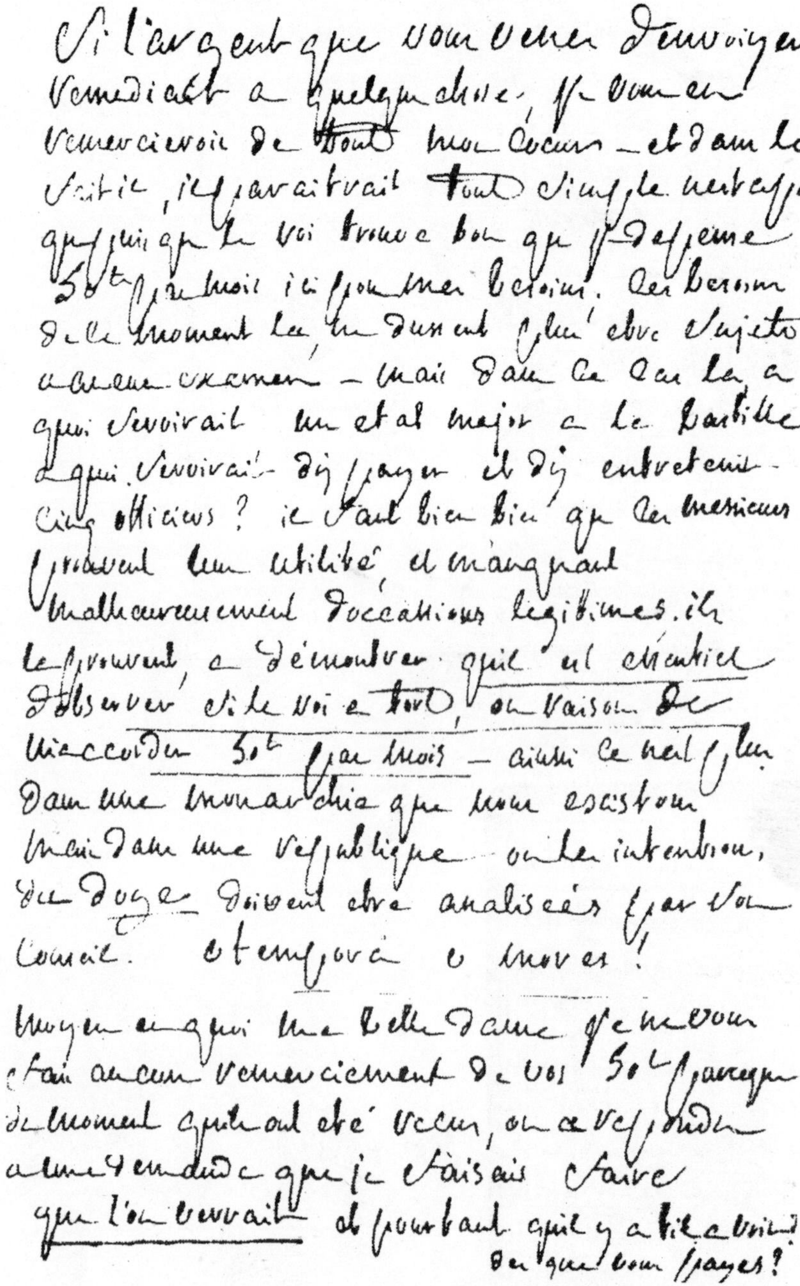
Si l'argent que vous venez d'envoyer
remediait a quelque chose, je vous en
remercierois de tout mon cœur — et dans le
fait, il paraitrait tout simple, n'est ce pas
que puisque le roi trouve bon que je depense
50 l par mois ici pour mes besoins, ces besoins
de ce moment la, ne devront plus etre sujets
a aucun examen — mais dans ce cas la a
quoi servirait un etat major a la bastille?
a quoi servirait de payer et d'entretenir
cinq officiers? il faut bien bien que ces messieurs
prouvent leur utilité, et manquant
malheureusement d'occassions legitimes, ils
le prouvent, a démontrer qu'il est essentiel
d'observer si le roi a tort, ou raison de
m'accorder 50 l par mois — ainsi ce n'est plus
dans une monarchie que nous existons
mais dans une republique ou les intentions
des doges doivent etre analisées par son
conseil. o tempora o mores!
moyennant quoi ma belle dame je ne vous
fais aucun remerciement de vos 50 l parce que
du moment qu'ils ont eté reçus, on a repondu
a une demande que je faisais faire
que l'on verrait et pourtant qu'il y a t'il a voir
des que vous payez?

The Marquis de Sade to his wife